Mastering Automobile Sales

The Ultimate Training Guide

By

Doug Hensley

Copyright 2024

ISBN 978-1-304-23515-2
Imprint: Lulu.com

Table of Contents

Chapter 1: Introduction to Automobile Sales

- Understanding the Automotive Sales Industry
- The Role of Sales Professionals
- Key Skills and Traits for Success

Chapter 2: Building Rapport and Trust with Customers

- Developing Effective Communication Skills
- Techniques for Building Customer Trust
- Establishing Long-Term Relationships

Chapter 3: Mastering Product Knowledge

- Understanding Vehicle Features and Specifications
- Highlighting Benefits and Unique Selling Points
- Staying Updated on Industry Trends

Chapter 4: Effective Sales Techniques and Strategies

- The Sales Process: Steps and Best Practices
- Overcoming Objections and Handling Rejections
- Closing Techniques and Negotiation Skills

Chapter 5: Digital Marketing Strategies for Automotive Sales

- Website Optimization and User Experience
- Search Engine Optimization (SEO) for Dealerships
- Pay-Per-Click (PPC) Advertising and Remarketing Strategies

Chapter 6: Social Media Marketing in Automotive Sales

- Leveraging Social Media Platforms for Brand Awareness
- Content Strategies for Engaging Automotive Customers
- Managing Online Reputation and Customer Feedback

Chapter 7: Finance and Insurance (F&I) Strategies in Automotive Sales

- Importance of F&I in Dealership Profitability
- Product Offerings: Financing Options and Insurance Products
- Compliance Considerations and Ethical Practices

Chapter 8: Customer Service Excellence in Automotive Sales

- Creating a Customer-Centric Culture
- Effective Communication Strategies
- Handling Customer Inquiries, Complaints, and Resolutions

Chapter 9: Service Department Excellence in Automotive Sales

- Optimizing Service Operations
- Service Advisor Roles and Responsibilities
- Technician Training and Technology Integration

Chapter 10: Quality Assurance and Continuous Improvement

- Monitoring Service Quality and Performance Metrics
- Managing Customer Expectations and Upselling Opportunities
- Fostering a Culture of Continuous Improvement

Chapter 11: Leadership and Team Development

- Leadership in Automotive Sales Management
- Building and Motivating Sales Teams
- Training and Development Programs for Sales Professionals

Chapter 12: Ethics and Professionalism in

Automobile Sales

- Ethical Considerations in Sales Practices
- Professional Standards and Codes of Conduct
- Handling Ethical Dilemmas and Difficult Situations

Chapter 13: Legal Aspects and Compliance in Automotive Sales

- Understanding Legal Requirements and Regulations
- Consumer Protection Laws and Dealership Responsibilities
- Compliance Training and Documentation Practices

Chapter 14: Future Trends in Automotive Sales

- Emerging Technologies and Their Impact on Sales
- Predictions for Automotive Market Trends
- Adaptation Strategies for Future Challenges

Chapter 15: Case Studies and Success Stories

- Real-World Examples of Successful Sales Strategies
- Analysis of Industry Innovations and Best Practices
- Lessons Learned from Top Performers in Automotive Sales

Chapter 16: Conclusion
- Recap of Key Learnings and Takeaways
- Looking Ahead: Opportunities and Challenges in Automotive Sales
- Final Thoughts on Excelling in the Automotive Sales Industry

Author's Notes

This book is dedicated to some of the Automotive professionals I have worked with in the past including Bill Lewin, Bill Clutter, Rich Ackman, Rob Marshall, Chris Hartsfield, Corey Taylor, Cale Barr, Jim Shell, Buck Walter, Randy Mann, Scottie

Hall and Todd Hudak, one of the best BDC and Sales Trainers in the business.

"Dive into the world of Automobile Sales Training, where expertise meets innovation and customer satisfaction drives success. This comprehensive guide takes you through every aspect of the automotive sales process, from mastering customer interactions and leveraging digital marketing strategies to navigating finance and insurance complexities and optimizing service department operations.

Learn essential skills such as building rapport, mastering product knowledge, and effective negotiation techniques. Discover how to harness the power of digital marketing, social media, and online reputation management to expand your dealership's reach and engage customers effectively.

Explore the critical role of finance and insurance (F&I) departments in closing deals and enhancing profitability, while ensuring compliance and ethical practices. Delve into the intricacies of delivering exceptional customer service, managing service departments, and fostering a culture of continuous improvement.

Packed with practical insights, case studies, and future trends, this book is your ultimate resource

Chapter 1: Introduction to Automobile Sales

The Evolution of Car Sales

Automobile sales have a rich history that reflects broader trends in consumer behavior, technological advancements, and economic shifts. Understanding this history provides context for modern sales strategies and highlights how the role of a car salesperson has evolved.

Early Days of Automobile Sales:

The early 20th century saw the birth of the automobile industry, with pioneers like Henry Ford revolutionizing production through the assembly line. Initially, cars were a luxury item, accessible only to the wealthy. Sales were conducted through direct contacts, with manufacturers like Ford and General Motors using traveling salesmen and small dealerships to reach potential buyers.

As mass production reduced costs, cars became more affordable, leading to a boom in demand. Dealerships began to proliferate, and the need for skilled salespeople grew. Early sales techniques were rudimentary, focusing on the novelty of the automobile and its potential to transform everyday life.

Post-War Boom and the Golden Age of Car

Sales:

After World War II, the automotive industry experienced unprecedented growth. The American economy was booming, suburbanization was on the rise, and car ownership became a symbol of freedom and status. Dealerships expanded, and the competition intensified. Sales strategies evolved to include promotional events, financing options, and trade-in programs.

This period also saw the rise of the "car salesman" archetype, often characterized by aggressive sales tactics. The focus was on high-pressure techniques to close deals quickly. However, this approach sometimes led to negative perceptions of car salespeople.

Modern Era and the Internet Revolution:

The advent of the internet in the late 20th century brought significant changes to automobile sales. Information became readily accessible, empowering consumers to research vehicles, compare prices, and read reviews before ever setting foot in a dealership. This shift necessitated a change in sales tactics from high-pressure techniques to a more consultative approach.

Dealerships began investing in online presence, and the role of the salesperson evolved to become more of a product specialist and customer advisor. Transparency and trust became crucial, as informed customers expected honest and knowledgeable guidance.

Current Trends and Future Directions:

Today, the automobile sales landscape is shaped by digital innovation, changing consumer preferences, and environmental considerations. Online sales platforms, virtual showrooms, and augmented reality experiences are becoming commonplace. Salespeople must be adept at using these technologies to engage customers and provide seamless buying experiences.

Moreover, the rise of electric vehicles (EVs) and autonomous driving technology is transforming the industry. Salespeople need to stay informed about these developments to educate and advise customers effectively.

The Role of a Car Salesperson:

A car salesperson's role is multifaceted, requiring a blend of interpersonal skills, product knowledge, and sales acumen. Let's break down the key aspects of this role:

Customer Relationship Management:

Building and maintaining relationships with customers is at the heart of automobile sales. This involves:

- **Understanding Customer Needs:** A good salesperson listens actively to understand what the customer is looking for, considering factors such as budget, lifestyle, and preferences.

- **Building Rapport and Trust:** Establishing a connection with the customer is crucial. This involves being personable, trustworthy, and empathetic.

- **Follow-Up and Retention:** Maintaining contact with customers after the sale is essential for long-term success. This can lead to repeat business and referrals.

Product Knowledge and Expertise:

Salespeople must have in-depth knowledge of the vehicles they sell, including:

- **Technical Specifications:** Understanding the features, performance, and capabilities of different models.

- **Comparative Knowledge:** Being able to compare different models and brands, highlighting the advantages of their offerings.

- **Staying Updated:** Keeping abreast of industry trends, new releases, and technological advancements.

Sales Techniques and Strategies:

Effective sales techniques are vital for success. Key strategies include:

- **Needs Assessment:** Conducting a thorough assessment to match the customer with the right vehicle.

- **Demonstration and Test Drives:** Effectively showcasing the vehicle's features and performance.

- **Handling Objections:** Addressing any concerns or objections the customer may have with confidence and clarity.

- **Closing the Deal:** Using various closing techniques to finalize the sale while ensuring the customer feels satisfied and valued.

The Importance of Sales Training:

Given the complexities of the role, ongoing training is essential for car salespeople. Training programs typically cover:

- **Sales Techniques and Processes:** Structured approaches to selling, from initial contact to closing the deal.

- **Product Knowledge:** Detailed information about the vehicles being sold, including technical specifications and unique selling points.

- **Customer Service Skills:** Training on how to interact with customers, build rapport, and handle various situations.

- **Technology and Tools:** Instruction on using CRM systems, online sales platforms, and other digital tools.

Ethical and Legal Considerations:

Ethics and legality are paramount in automobile sales. Salespeople must:

- **Adhere to Legal Requirements:** Understanding and complying with regulations related to sales contracts, financing, and consumer rights.
- **Promote Ethical Sales Practices:** Ensuring transparency, honesty, and fairness in all dealings.

Challenges and Opportunities in Automobile Sales:

While the role of a car salesperson can be rewarding, it also comes with challenges, including:

- **Competition:** The automotive market is highly competitive, requiring salespeople to differentiate themselves and their products.
- **Economic Fluctuations:** Economic conditions can significantly impact car sales, necessitating adaptability and resilience.
- **Technological Advancements:** Staying updated with rapid technological changes

can be challenging but also provides opportunities for innovation.

Conclusion:

The role of a car salesperson is dynamic and multifaceted, requiring a blend of interpersonal skills, product knowledge, and adaptability. As the automotive industry continues to evolve, ongoing training and a commitment to ethical practices will be key to success in this field.

The Importance of Sales Training

Sales training is a crucial element in the success of any automobile salesperson. It equips salespeople with the skills, knowledge, and confidence needed to excel in a competitive market. Let's delve deeper into why sales training is so important and what it typically involves.

Enhancing Product Knowledge:

A thorough understanding of the vehicles being sold is fundamental. Training ensures that salespeople are knowledgeable about:

- **Technical Specifications:** Understanding engine types, performance metrics, safety features, and other technical details.

- **Unique Selling Points:** Knowing what sets their vehicles apart from competitors, whether it's innovative technology, superior safety ratings, or exceptional fuel efficiency.

- **Latest Models and Trends:** Staying updated on the newest models and automotive trends, including electric vehicles and autonomous driving features.

Improving Sales Techniques:

Effective sales techniques are essential for converting prospects into customers. Training covers:

- **Sales Process Mastery:** From greeting the customer to closing the sale, understanding each step of the sales process.

- **Handling Objections:** Learning strategies to address common objections and concerns, turning potential deal-breakers into opportunities.

- **Closing Techniques:** Mastering various closing techniques, such as the assumptive close, the urgency close, and the alternative choice close.

Developing Interpersonal Skills:

Building strong relationships with customers is key to long-term success. Training in this area focuses on:

- **Effective Communication:** Developing listening skills, asking the right questions, and conveying information clearly and persuasively.

- **Building Rapport:** Techniques for establishing trust and a positive relationship with customers.

- **Customer Service Excellence:** Ensuring a high level of customer satisfaction, both during and after the sale.

Utilizing Technology:

Modern sales training includes the use of technology to enhance the sales process. This involves:

- **CRM Systems:** Training on how to use Customer Relationship Management systems to track leads, manage customer interactions, and follow up effectively.

- **Digital Marketing:** Understanding how to leverage social media, email marketing, and other digital tools to generate leads and engage with customers.

- **Online Sales Platforms:** Navigating and utilizing online sales platforms to reach a broader audience and provide a seamless buying experience.

Ethical and Legal Training:

Maintaining ethical standards and adhering to legal requirements is crucial. Training in this area includes:

- **Understanding Regulations:** Familiarity with laws and regulations related to automobile sales, including financing and consumer protection laws.
- **Promoting Ethical Behavior:** Encouraging transparency, honesty, and fairness in all sales interactions.
- **Handling Sensitive Information:** Training on the proper handling of customer data and maintaining confidentiality.

Building Confidence and Motivation:

Sales training also focuses on personal development, helping salespeople build confidence and stay motivated. This includes:

- **Goal Setting:** Training on how to set and achieve sales goals, both short-term and long-term.
- **Overcoming Rejection:** Techniques for dealing with rejection and maintaining a positive attitude.
- **Continuous Learning:** Encouraging a mindset of continuous improvement and lifelong learning.

Case Studies and Real-World Scenarios:

Training programs often include case studies and

real-world scenarios to provide practical experience. This helps salespeople:

- **Apply Theory to Practice:** Understanding how to apply sales techniques and strategies in real-life situations.

- **Learn from Experience:** Analyzing successful and unsuccessful sales interactions to learn what works and what doesn't.

- **Improve Problem-Solving Skills:** Developing the ability to think on their feet and handle unexpected challenges.

The ROI of Sales Training:

Investing in sales training yields significant returns for both the salesperson and the dealership. Benefits include:

- **Increased Sales:** Well-trained salespeople are more effective at closing deals, leading to higher sales volumes.

- **Customer Satisfaction:** Providing excellent service results in happier customers, leading to repeat business and referrals.

- **Employee Retention:** Salespeople who feel supported and equipped with the necessary skills are more likely to stay with the dealership long-term.

- **Brand Reputation:** Ethical and knowledgeable sales practices enhance

Chapter 2: Building a Solid Foundation

Building a solid foundation is crucial for success in automobile sales. This chapter will delve deeply into the elements that form the bedrock of a successful career in this field, including developing the right mindset, building confidence and resilience, acquiring comprehensive product knowledge, and understanding different types of vehicles.

Developing a Sales Mindset

A successful automobile salesperson starts with the right mindset. This involves cultivating a positive attitude, staying motivated, and being goal-oriented. Here are key aspects to consider:

Positive Attitude:

A positive attitude is essential in sales, where rejection and challenges are part of the daily routine. Salespeople must maintain a positive outlook to stay motivated and inspire confidence in their customers.

- **Self-Talk and Affirmations:** Using positive self-talk and daily affirmations can help salespeople maintain a positive mindset. Phrases like "I am capable of closing deals" or "I am an expert in my field" can reinforce self-belief.

- **Visualizing Success:** Visualization techniques involve picturing successful sales interactions and outcomes. This mental rehearsal can boost confidence and prepare salespeople for real-life scenarios.
- **Gratitude Practices:** Focusing on the positive aspects of each day and expressing gratitude can help salespeople maintain a positive attitude, even in the face of challenges.

Staying Motivated:

Motivation drives salespeople to achieve their goals and continuously improve their performance. Different strategies can be employed to maintain high levels of motivation:

- **Setting Personal Goals:** Salespeople should set both short-term and long-term goals. Short-term goals could include daily or weekly sales targets, while long-term goals might involve career advancement or earning a certain income level.
- **Reward Systems:** Creating a personal reward system can provide motivation. For example, a salesperson might reward themselves with a treat or a day off after reaching a sales milestone.

- **Peer Support:** Surrounding oneself with motivated colleagues and engaging in team activities can foster a supportive and competitive environment that boosts motivation.

Being Goal-Oriented:

Having clear, achievable goals is crucial for success in sales. Goal-setting provides direction and a sense of purpose.

- **SMART Goals:** Goals should be Specific, Measurable, Achievable, Relevant, and Time-bound. For example, "Increase monthly sales by 20% within the next three months" is a SMART goal.

- **Action Plans:** Developing detailed action plans to achieve goals ensures that salespeople stay focused and organized. This might include daily tasks, customer follow-ups, and targeted prospecting activities.

- **Regular Review and Adjustment:** Goals should be reviewed regularly to track progress and make necessary adjustments. This helps in staying aligned with long-term objectives.

Building Confidence and Resilience

Confidence and resilience are key traits for any

successful salesperson. These qualities help in handling rejection, bouncing back from setbacks, and maintaining a consistent performance.

Building Confidence:

Confidence stems from competence and self-belief. Here are strategies to build confidence in automobile sales:

- **Mastering Product Knowledge:** Knowing the products inside and out instills confidence. Salespeople should regularly study vehicle specifications, features, and benefits.

- **Role-Playing and Practice:** Engaging in role-playing exercises with colleagues or mentors can simulate real sales scenarios, helping salespeople practice their pitch and refine their approach.

- **Seeking Feedback:** Constructive feedback from managers and peers can highlight areas for improvement and reinforce strengths, boosting confidence.

Developing Resilience:

Resilience is the ability to recover quickly from difficulties. In sales, this means not being deterred by rejection or setbacks.

- **Mindfulness and Stress Management:** Techniques such as mindfulness, meditation, and deep breathing exercises can help manage stress and maintain focus.

- **Adopting a Growth Mindset:** Viewing challenges as opportunities for growth rather than obstacles fosters resilience. Salespeople with a growth mindset are more likely to learn from their experiences and persist in the face of difficulties.
- **Support Systems:** Having a strong support system, whether it's colleagues, friends, or family, provides emotional support and encouragement during tough times.

Importance of Product Knowledge

In-depth product knowledge is a cornerstone of successful automobile sales. Salespeople must be well-versed in the vehicles they sell to provide accurate information and build customer trust.

Understanding Technical Specifications:

Salespeople should have a thorough understanding of the technical aspects of their vehicles, including:

- **Engine Types and Performance:** Knowing the differences between various engine types (e.g., gasoline, diesel, hybrid, electric) and their performance characteristics.
- **Safety Features:** Understanding the safety

features of each vehicle, such as airbags, anti-lock braking systems, and advanced driver-assistance systems (ADAS).

- **Technology and Infotainment:** Being familiar with the latest technology and infotainment systems, including navigation, connectivity, and driver assistance features.

Highlighting Unique Selling Points:

Each vehicle has unique features and benefits that set it apart from competitors. Salespeople should be able to highlight these points effectively:

- **Fuel Efficiency:** Emphasizing the fuel efficiency of a vehicle can be a strong selling point for cost-conscious customers.

- **Design and Comfort:** Discussing the design elements and comfort features, such as interior materials, seating configurations, and ergonomics, can appeal to customers looking for luxury and convenience.

- **Performance and Handling:** Highlighting the performance aspects, such as acceleration, handling, and ride quality, can attract customers who prioritize driving experience.

Staying Updated:

The automotive industry is constantly evolving, with new models and technologies being introduced regularly. Salespeople must stay updated:

- **Ongoing Training:** Participating in regular training sessions and workshops to keep abreast of new developments.
- **Manufacturer Resources:** Utilizing resources provided by manufacturers, such as product manuals, training videos, and webinars.
- **Industry Publications:** Reading industry magazines, websites, and blogs to stay informed about the latest trends and innovations.

Understanding Different Types of Vehicles

Salespeople need to understand the various types of vehicles available in the market to match customers with the right options. Here's a breakdown of different vehicle types:

Sedans:

Sedans are popular for their practicality and comfort. Key points include:

- **Variety of Sizes:** Sedans come in various sizes, including compact, mid-size, and full-size, catering to different customer needs.
- **Balance of Performance and Efficiency:**

Sedans often offer a good balance between performance and fuel efficiency, making them suitable for daily commuting.

- **Comfort and Features:** Emphasize the comfort, safety features, and technology options available in sedans.

SUVs and Crossovers:

SUVs and crossovers have gained popularity for their versatility and spaciousness. Key points include:

- **Different Sizes and Configurations:** Understanding the differences between compact, mid-size, and full-size SUVs, as well as crossovers.

- **All-Wheel Drive and Off-Road Capabilities:** Highlighting the all-wheel drive options and off-road capabilities for customers who prioritize adventure and utility.

- **Cargo Space and Passenger Comfort:** Emphasizing the ample cargo space and comfortable seating for families and those needing extra room.

Trucks:

Trucks are favored for their power and utility. Key points include:

- **Engine and Towing Capabilities:**

Understanding the different engine options and towing capacities, which are crucial for customers needing a vehicle for heavy-duty tasks.

- **Bed Sizes and Configurations:** Explaining the various bed sizes and configurations available, as well as additional features like bed liners and cargo management systems.

- **Off-Road and Work Features:** Highlighting off-road capabilities and features designed for work, such as integrated trailer brake controllers and rugged suspension systems.

Electric Vehicles (EVs):

EVs are becoming increasingly important as the automotive industry shifts towards sustainability. Key points include:

- **Battery Range and Charging:** Understanding the battery range of different EV models and the availability of charging infrastructure.

- **Environmental Benefits:** Emphasizing the environmental benefits of driving an EV, such as reduced emissions and lower operating costs.

- **Technology and Incentives:** Discussing the advanced technology features often found in EVs, as well as any government incentives or tax credits available.

Hybrid Vehicles:

Hybrids offer a combination of traditional internal combustion engines and electric power. Key points include:

- **Fuel Efficiency:** Highlighting the improved fuel efficiency compared to conventional gasoline vehicles.

- **Regenerative Braking:** Explaining how regenerative braking works and its benefits for energy efficiency.

- **Range and Performance:** Discussing the driving range and performance characteristics of hybrid vehicles.

Luxury Vehicles:

Luxury vehicles are designed for customers seeking high-end features and superior performance. Key points include:

- **Premium Materials and Craftsmanship:** Emphasizing the use of premium materials, advanced technology, and superior craftsmanship.

- **Performance and Handling:** Highlighting the performance capabilities, including powerful engines, advanced suspension systems, and precise handling.

- **Exclusive Features:** Discussing exclusive features such as advanced driver assistance systems, high-end infotainment systems, and customizable options.

Commercial Vehicles:

Commercial vehicles are designed for business use and include vans, trucks, and specialty vehicles. Key points include:

- **Utility and Capacity:** Understanding the utility and cargo capacity requirements of different businesses.

- **Customization Options:** Discussing customization options available for specific business needs, such as shelving, refrigeration units, and branding.

- **Durability and Reliability:** Emphasizing the durability and reliability required for commercial use, including maintenance and service options.

Conclusion

Building a solid foundation in automobile sales involves developing the right mindset, building confidence and resilience, acquiring comprehensive product knowledge, and understanding different types of vehicles. By mastering these elements, salespeople can position themselves for long-term success in the competitive and ever-evolving automotive industry.

Chapter 3: Mastering Communication Skills

Effective communication is the cornerstone of successful automobile sales. Mastering communication skills helps salespeople build rapport with customers, understand their needs, and convey information clearly and persuasively. This chapter delves into the art of listening, asking the right questions, building rapport and trust, and mastering both verbal and non-verbal communication.

The Art of Listening

Listening is a fundamental skill in sales. It allows salespeople to understand their customers' needs and preferences, build rapport, and tailor their approach accordingly. Here are some key aspects of effective listening:

Active Listening:

Active listening involves fully concentrating, understanding, responding, and remembering what the customer says. This goes beyond merely hearing words; it requires engagement and interaction.

- **Eye Contact:** Maintaining eye contact shows that you are focused and interested in what the customer is saying.

- **Nodding and Affirmations:** Using small gestures like nodding and verbal affirmations (e.g., "I see," "I understand") signals that you are paying attention.
- **Avoiding Interruptions:** Allowing the customer to speak without interrupting demonstrates respect and patience.

Reflective Listening:

Reflective listening involves paraphrasing or summarizing what the customer has said to ensure understanding and show that you are listening.

- **Paraphrasing:** Restate the customer's words in your own words to confirm understanding. For example, "So, you're looking for a car with good fuel efficiency and enough space for your family, is that right?"
- **Summarizing:** Provide a brief summary of the key points the customer has mentioned. This helps to clarify and confirm important details.

Empathic Listening:

Empathic listening involves understanding and sharing the feelings of the customer. It builds deeper connections and trust.

- **Showing Empathy:** Express empathy by

acknowledging the customer's emotions and concerns. For example, "I understand that safety is a top priority for you, especially with young children."

- **Mirroring Emotions:** Reflect the customer's emotions in your responses to show that you genuinely understand their feelings.

Listening for Cues:

Listening for verbal and non-verbal cues helps salespeople pick up on unspoken needs and preferences.

- **Tone of Voice:** Pay attention to the customer's tone of voice to gauge their level of interest, enthusiasm, or hesitation.
- **Body Language:** Observe the customer's body language for additional insights into their thoughts and feelings.

Asking the Right Questions

Asking the right questions is essential for uncovering customer needs, guiding the conversation, and providing appropriate solutions. Here are various types of questions and how to use them effectively:

Open-Ended Questions:

Open-ended questions encourage the customer to

share more information and provide detailed responses. They typically begin with "how," "what," "why," or "describe."

- **Examples:**
  - "What are you looking for in your next vehicle?"
  - "How do you plan to use this car on a daily basis?"
  - "Why is fuel efficiency important to you?"

Closed-Ended Questions:

Closed-ended questions elicit short, specific answers, often "yes" or "no." They are useful for confirming details and narrowing down options.

- **Examples:**
  - "Do you prefer an SUV or a sedan?"
  - "Is a sunroof a must-have feature for you?"
  - "Would you like to schedule a test drive this weekend?"

Probing Questions:

Probing questions dig deeper into the customer's responses to gain more insight. They help clarify and expand on initial answers.

- **Examples:**
  - "Can you tell me more about your previous car and what you liked

about it?"
- "What specific features are you looking for in terms of safety?"
- "Could you explain why you prefer a hybrid vehicle?"

Clarifying Questions:

Clarifying questions ensure that you and the customer are on the same page. They help avoid misunderstandings and confirm details.

- **Examples:**
  - "When you say you need a lot of cargo space, do you have a specific amount in mind?"
  - "You mentioned wanting advanced technology—are you referring to the infotainment system or driver assistance features?"
  - "Just to confirm, are you planning to finance or lease the vehicle?"

Leading Questions:

Leading questions subtly guide the customer towards a particular conclusion or decision. They can be useful for steering the conversation but should be used carefully to avoid appearing manipulative.

- **Examples:**
  - "Wouldn't you agree that the extra safety features of this model are

worth the investment?"
- "Don't you think this color looks great with the interior design?"
- "Isn't it reassuring to know that this vehicle comes with a comprehensive warranty?"

Hypothetical Questions:

Hypothetical questions encourage the customer to imagine scenarios and consider how a particular feature or vehicle would fit into their life.

- **Examples:**
    - "If you were to take a long road trip, how important would comfort and infotainment features be?"
    - "How would you feel knowing that your new car has top-of-the-line safety ratings?"
    - "Imagine having the convenience of keyless entry and push-button start—how would that enhance your daily routine?"

Building Rapport and Trust

Building rapport and trust is crucial for establishing a positive relationship with the customer. When customers feel comfortable and trust the salesperson, they are more likely to share their true needs and make a purchase.

Establishing Common Ground:

Finding common ground with the customer helps to build a connection. This could be shared interests, experiences, or values.

- **Personal Connections:** Engage in small talk to discover common interests or backgrounds. For example, "I see you're a sports fan—what's your favorite team?"
- **Shared Experiences:** Relate to the customer's experiences. For example, "I recently took a similar road trip with my family, and I found that having extra cargo space was really beneficial."

Showing Genuine Interest:

Showing genuine interest in the customer as a person, not just a potential sale, fosters trust and rapport.

- **Active Listening:** Demonstrate that you are truly interested in what the customer is saying by listening attentively and asking follow-up questions.
- **Personalized Attention:** Tailor your approach to each customer based on their unique needs and preferences. Avoid using a one-size-fits-all script.

Being Honest and Transparent:

Honesty and transparency are fundamental to

building trust. Customers appreciate when salespeople are upfront about all aspects of the sale.

- **Clear Information:** Provide clear and accurate information about the vehicles, pricing, and financing options.

- **Admitting Uncertainties:** If you don't know the answer to a question, admit it and commit to finding the information. For example, "I'm not sure about that specific detail, but I'll find out for you right away."

- **Addressing Concerns:** Address any concerns or objections the customer has openly and honestly. Avoid downplaying or dismissing their worries.

Consistency and Reliability:

Consistency and reliability build long-term trust with customers. Salespeople should follow through on promises and maintain consistent communication.

- **Follow-Up:** Regularly follow up with customers to provide updates, answer questions, and show that you value their business.

- **Keeping Promises:** If you promise to call a customer back or provide additional information, ensure that you do so promptly and reliably.

Professionalism and Courtesy:

Professionalism and courtesy are essential for creating a positive impression and building trust.

- **Respectful Communication:** Always communicate with customers in a respectful and courteous manner. Avoid interrupting, arguing, or using overly casual language.

- **Professional Appearance:** Dress and present yourself in a professional manner. A neat and tidy appearance reflects positively on you and your dealership.

Effective Verbal Communication

Effective verbal communication is key to conveying information clearly and persuasively. This includes both the words you choose and the way you deliver them.

Clarity and Simplicity:

Clear and simple language helps customers understand your message without confusion.

- **Avoid Jargon:** Use straightforward language and avoid industry jargon that the customer may not understand. For example, instead of saying "This car has a turbocharged engine with direct injection," you could say "This car has a powerful engine that provides quick acceleration and better fuel efficiency."

- **Concise Explanations:** Keep your explanations concise and to the point. Avoid overloading the customer with too much information at once.

Persuasive Language:

Persuasive language encourages customers to see the benefits of the vehicles and make a purchase decision.

- **Highlight Benefits:** Focus on the benefits of the features you describe. For example, instead of saying "This car has a sunroof," you could say "This sunroof lets in plenty of natural light, making your drives more enjoyable."

- **Use Positive Language:** Frame your statements positively. For example, instead of saying "This model is not as expensive as others," say "This model offers great value for its price."

Tone and Pace:

The tone and pace of your speech impact how your message is received.

- **Friendly and Professional Tone:** Maintain a friendly yet professional tone to create a positive and respectful interaction.

- **Pacing:** Speak at a moderate pace to ensure that the customer can follow your explanations. Avoid speaking too quickly, which can overwhelm the customer, or too slowly, which can lose their interest.

Storytelling:

Storytelling is a powerful tool in sales. Sharing relevant stories can make your message more engaging and relatable.

- **Customer Stories:** Share stories of previous customers who had similar needs and how the vehicle met those needs. For example, "I had a customer last month who was also looking for a family car, and they found that this model provided the perfect blend of space and comfort."
- **Personal Experiences:** Share your own experiences with the vehicles. For example, "I recently drove this model on a road trip, and I was impressed by the smooth ride and fuel efficiency."

Mastering Non-Verbal Communication

Non-verbal communication, such as body language, facial expressions, and gestures, plays a significant role in how your message is perceived.

Body Language:

Positive body language helps create a welcoming and trustworthy atmosphere.

- **Open Posture:** Maintain an open posture with arms relaxed and uncrossed. This conveys openness and approachability.
- **Leaning Forward:** Leaning slightly forward when the customer is speaking shows interest and engagement.
- **Personal Space:** Respect the customer's personal space. Avoid standing too close, which can make them feel uncomfortable.

Facial Expressions:

Facial expressions convey emotions and reactions.

- **Smiling:** A genuine smile creates a friendly and welcoming impression.
- **Nodding:** Nodding while the customer is speaking signals agreement and understanding.
- **Eye Contact:** Maintaining appropriate eye contact shows confidence and attentiveness.

Gestures:

Gestures can reinforce your verbal messages and make your communication more dynamic.

- **Hand Gestures:** Use hand gestures to emphasize key points. For example, you can gesture to indicate the size of the vehicle or highlight a feature.

- **Pointing and Demonstrating:** Pointing to specific features on the vehicle and demonstrating how they work helps make your explanations more tangible.

Mirroring:

Mirroring involves subtly mimicking the customer's body language and speech patterns. This can help build rapport and make the customer feel more comfortable.

- **Subtle Mirroring:** Mirror the customer's posture, gestures, and tone of voice in a subtle and natural way. For example, if the customer is speaking softly, you can lower your voice slightly to match their tone.

- **Pacing and Leading:** Start by mirroring the customer's body language and gradually lead them towards a more positive and open posture.

Handling Objections

Handling objections is a critical skill in sales. Objections are natural and should be seen as opportunities to address concerns and provide additional information.

Anticipating Objections:

Anticipate common objections and prepare responses in advance.

- **Common Objections:** Common objections might include price concerns, feature preferences, or doubts about the brand. Prepare clear and concise responses to address these issues.

- **Empathy and Understanding:** Show empathy and understanding when the customer raises an objection. For example, "I understand that the price might seem high, but let me explain the value and benefits you're getting."

Responding to Objections:

Respond to objections in a positive and constructive manner.

- **Listen and Acknowledge:** Listen carefully to the customer's objection and acknowledge their concern. For example, "I hear that you're concerned about the fuel efficiency."

- **Provide Information:** Provide additional information or clarification to address the objection. For example, "This model actually has a very efficient engine that provides great fuel economy for its class."

- **Offer Solutions:** Offer solutions or alternatives that meet the customer's needs.

For example, "If fuel efficiency is a top priority, we also have a hybrid model that you might find interesting."

Reframing Objections:

Reframe objections as opportunities to highlight the benefits and advantages of the vehicle.

- **Turn Negatives into Positives:** Reframe negative aspects as positive features. For example, if the customer is concerned about the size of the vehicle, you could say, "While it may seem large, this SUV offers excellent visibility and a comfortable ride for the whole family."

- **Highlight Value:** Emphasize the value and benefits of the vehicle in response to objections. For example, "I understand that the price is a consideration, but this model includes many advanced safety features and a comprehensive warranty."

Closing Techniques:

Effective closing techniques help guide the customer towards making a purchase decision.

- **Assumptive Close:** Assume that the customer is ready to buy and move towards the next steps. For example, "Let's get the paperwork started so you can drive your new car home today."

- **Summary Close:** Summarize the key benefits and features discussed to reinforce the value of the vehicle. For example, "To recap, this car offers excellent fuel efficiency, advanced safety features, and a spacious interior—everything you mentioned was important to you."

- **Direct Close:** Ask directly for the sale in a confident and respectful manner. For example, "Are you ready to move forward with this purchase?"

Conclusion

Mastering communication skills is essential for success in automobile sales. By developing effective listening techniques, asking the right questions, building rapport and trust, and honing both verbal and non-verbal communication, salespeople can create positive interactions, address customer needs, and guide them towards making informed purchase decisions. Effective communication not only enhances sales performance but also fosters long-term customer relationships and satisfaction.

Chapter 4: Understanding the Sales Process

The sales process in the automotive industry is a

structured journey that both the salesperson and the customer embark on together. It is essential for sales professionals to understand each stage of this process in detail to guide the customer seamlessly from the initial inquiry to the final purchase. This chapter will explore the sales process comprehensively, covering everything from the initial contact to post-sale follow-up.

The Stages of the Sales Process
1. **Prospecting and Lead Generation**
2. **Initial Contact**
3. **Qualifying the Lead**
4. **Needs Assessment**
5. **Presentation and Demonstration**
6. **Handling Objections**
7. **Closing the Sale**
8. **Post-Sale Follow-Up**

1. Prospecting and Lead Generation

Prospecting is the process of identifying potential customers who may be interested in purchasing a vehicle. This is the foundation of the sales process, as it ensures a steady stream of potential buyers.

Lead Generation involves strategies to attract and capture the interest of potential customers.

Traditional Methods:
- **Cold Calling:** Contacting potential

customers by phone to introduce yourself and your dealership.
- **Direct Mail:** Sending promotional materials or offers directly to potential customers' homes.
- **Networking:** Building relationships with individuals and organizations in the community to generate referrals.

Digital Methods:

- **Social Media Marketing:** Utilizing platforms like Facebook, Instagram, and Twitter to engage with potential customers and generate leads.
- **Email Campaigns:** Sending targeted emails to a list of potential customers with information about new models, promotions, and events.
- **SEO and SEM:** Optimizing your dealership's website for search engines and using paid search advertising to attract online visitors.

Events and Promotions:

- **Trade Shows and Exhibitions:** Participating in automotive trade shows to showcase vehicles and connect with potential customers.
- **In-Store Events:** Hosting events at the dealership, such as new model launches, test drive events, and customer appreciation

days.
- **Sponsorships:** Sponsoring local events or sports teams to increase brand visibility and attract potential customers.

Lead Management:

Effective lead management involves tracking and nurturing leads to convert them into sales.

- **CRM Systems:** Using Customer Relationship Management (CRM) software to track and manage leads, follow up with potential customers, and analyze data to improve lead generation strategies.
- **Lead Scoring:** Assigning scores to leads based on their likelihood to convert, allowing salespeople to prioritize high-potential leads.

2. Initial Contact

The initial contact is the first direct interaction between the salesperson and the potential customer. This stage sets the tone for the entire sales process.

Greeting and Introduction:

- **Professional and Friendly Greeting:** Approach the customer with a warm and professional greeting. For example, "Hello, welcome to [Dealership Name]. My name is [Your Name], and I'm here to assist you

today."
- **Initial Rapport Building:** Engage in small talk to create a comfortable atmosphere. Ask about their day or interests to establish a personal connection.

Establishing Trust:

- **Active Listening:** Show genuine interest in the customer's needs and concerns by listening attentively and asking open-ended questions.
- **Transparency:** Be honest and transparent about the sales process and what the customer can expect. This builds trust and sets the foundation for a positive relationship.

Identifying Customer Intent:

- **Inquiry About Needs:** Ask questions to understand the customer's intent. For example, "Are you looking for a new or pre-owned vehicle?" or "Do you have any specific models in mind?"
- **Assessing Urgency:** Determine the urgency of the customer's purchase decision. For example, "Are you planning to purchase a vehicle soon, or are you just gathering information at this stage?"

3. Qualifying the Lead

Qualifying the lead involves determining whether the potential customer is a serious buyer and assessing their buying criteria.

Identifying Buying Signals:

- **Interest in Test Drives:** A customer interested in scheduling a test drive is showing a strong buying signal.
- **Questions About Financing:** Inquiries about financing options, trade-ins, and monthly payments indicate a serious buyer.
- **Engagement Level:** Customers who are actively engaged, asking detailed questions, and showing enthusiasm are likely qualified leads.

Assessing Budget and Financing:

- **Budget Inquiry:** Ask about the customer's budget to ensure that you are presenting vehicles within their price range. For example, "What is your budget for this purchase?"
- **Financing Needs:** Determine if the customer needs financing and discuss available options. For example, "Are you planning to finance the vehicle or pay in full?"

Understanding Decision-Making Process:

- **Primary Decision-Maker:** Identify who the primary decision-maker is if the customer is accompanied by others. For example, "Who will be making the final decision on this purchase?"
- **Timeline for Purchase:** Ask about the customer's timeline for making a purchase. For example, "When are you looking to make a decision?"

4. Needs Assessment

Conducting a thorough needs assessment is crucial to understanding the customer's requirements and preferences.

Lifestyle and Usage:

- **Daily Commute:** Ask about the customer's daily commute and how they plan to use the vehicle. For example, "How many miles do you typically drive each day?"
- **Family and Cargo Needs:** Inquire about the customer's family size and cargo space requirements. For example, "Do you need a vehicle with ample cargo space for family trips?"

Feature Preferences:

- **Must-Have Features:** Identify the features that are most important to the customer. For example, "What are the must-have features

you're looking for in a vehicle?"
- **Technology and Safety:** Ask about the customer's preferences for technology and safety features. For example, "Are there any specific safety features or technology options you're interested in?"

Brand and Model Preferences:

- **Brand Loyalty:** Determine if the customer has a preference for a particular brand or model. For example, "Are you loyal to any specific brand, or are you open to different options?"
- **Previous Vehicles:** Ask about the customer's previous vehicles and their experiences. For example, "What did you like or dislike about your previous vehicle?"

Environmental Concerns:

- **Fuel Efficiency:** Inquire about the customer's preference for fuel-efficient or eco-friendly vehicles. For example, "How important is fuel efficiency to you?"
- **Electric and Hybrid Options:** Discuss electric and hybrid vehicle options if the customer is environmentally conscious. For example, "Would you be interested in exploring our electric or hybrid models?"

5. Presentation and Demonstration

The presentation and demonstration stage involves showcasing the vehicles that meet the customer's needs and preferences.

Selecting the Right Vehicles:

- **Matching Criteria:** Present vehicles that match the customer's criteria based on the needs assessment. For example, "Based on what you've shared, I think these models would be a great fit for you."
- **Highlighting Features:** Emphasize the features and benefits that align with the customer's preferences. For example, "This model has the advanced safety features you mentioned were important to you."

Conducting a Vehicle Walkaround:

- **Exterior Features:** Highlight key exterior features such as design, headlights, wheels, and storage compartments. For example, "As you can see, this model has a sleek design and LED headlights for better visibility."
- **Interior Features:** Showcase the interior features, including seating comfort, dashboard layout, and technology options. For example, "Inside, you'll find comfortable leather seats and a user-friendly infotainment system."

Demonstrating Technology:

- **Infotainment Systems:** Demonstrate how to use the infotainment system, including navigation, audio, and connectivity features. For example, "This system allows you to connect your smartphone for hands-free calling and access to your favorite apps."
- **Safety Features:** Explain and demonstrate advanced safety features such as adaptive cruise control, lane-keeping assist, and parking sensors. For example, "This vehicle is equipped with adaptive cruise control, which maintains a safe distance from the car in front of you."

Test Drives:

- **Scheduling Test Drives:** Encourage the customer to schedule a test drive to experience the vehicle firsthand. For example, "Would you like to take this car for a test drive to see how it feels on the road?"
- **Test Drive Route:** Plan a test drive route that allows the customer to experience various driving conditions, such as city streets and highways.
- **Accompanying the Customer:** Accompany the customer during the test drive to answer questions and highlight

features. For example, "Notice how smoothly the car accelerates and how quiet the cabin is."

6. Handling Objections

Handling objections is a crucial part of the sales process. It involves addressing the customer's concerns and providing solutions.

Common Objections:

- **Price Concerns:** Customers may have concerns about the price or affordability. For example, "I think this car is a bit out of my budget."
- **Feature Preferences:** Customers may have specific feature preferences that the vehicle doesn't meet. For example, "I was hoping for a car with a sunroof."
- **Brand or Model Concerns:** Customers may have concerns about the brand or model based on their past experiences or perceptions. For example, "I've heard mixed reviews about this brand's reliability."

Addressing Price Concerns:

- **Value Justification:** Emphasize the value and benefits the customer will receive for the price. For example, "This car comes with a comprehensive warranty and top-of-

the-line safety features, making it a great value for the price."
- **Flexible Financing:** Discuss flexible financing options to make the purchase more affordable. For example, "We offer various financing plans that can fit within your budget."

Overcoming Feature Objections:

- **Alternative Options:** Suggest alternative models or configurations that meet the customer's feature preferences. For example, "If a sunroof is important to you, we have another model that includes this feature."
- **Customization:** Discuss customization options or aftermarket accessories to meet the customer's needs. For example, "We can install a sunroof as an aftermarket accessory if you'd like."

Reassuring Brand Concerns:

- **Reliability and Reviews:** Provide information on the brand's reliability and positive customer reviews. For example, "This brand has received high ratings for reliability and customer satisfaction."
- **Warranty and Service:** Highlight the warranty and service packages that provide peace of mind. For example, "This car comes with a 5-year warranty and

complimentary maintenance for the first year."

7. Closing the Sale

Closing the sale involves finalizing the transaction and securing the customer's commitment to purchase.

Closing Techniques:

- **Assumptive Close:** Assume the customer is ready to buy and proceed with the next steps. For example, "Let's get the paperwork started so you can take your new car home today."
- **Summary Close:** Summarize the key benefits and features to reinforce the value of the vehicle. For example, "To recap, this car offers excellent fuel efficiency, advanced safety features, and a comfortable interior."
- **Direct Close:** Ask directly for the sale in a confident manner. For example, "Are you ready to move forward with this purchase?"

Negotiation Strategies:

- **Understanding Needs:** Focus on understanding the customer's needs and finding a mutually beneficial solution. For example, "Let's find a financing option that works for both of us."

- **Flexibility:** Be flexible and open to negotiation on price, financing terms, or additional features. For example, "We can offer you a special discount or include additional features to make this deal more attractive."

Finalizing Paperwork:

- **Accurate Documentation:** Ensure all necessary paperwork is completed accurately and thoroughly. This includes the purchase agreement, financing documents, and any trade-in paperwork.
- **Reviewing Terms:** Review the terms of the sale with the customer, including pricing, financing terms, and warranty information. For example, "Let's go over the final terms of your purchase to ensure everything is in order."

8. Post-Sale Follow-Up

Post-sale follow-up is essential for maintaining customer satisfaction and fostering long-term relationships.

Thank You and Appreciation:

- **Thank You Notes:** Send a personalized thank you note to express appreciation for the customer's business. For example, "Thank you for choosing [Dealership

Name]. We appreciate your business and look forward to serving you again."
- **Follow-Up Calls:** Make a follow-up call to check in with the customer and address any questions or concerns. For example, "I wanted to check in and see how you're enjoying your new car."

Customer Satisfaction:

- **Feedback and Reviews:** Ask for feedback and encourage the customer to leave a review of their experience. For example, "We value your feedback and would appreciate it if you could leave a review of your experience with us."
- **Addressing Issues:** Promptly address any issues or concerns the customer may have. For example, "If you encounter any issues with your vehicle, please let us know, and we'll be happy to assist."

Building Long-Term Relationships:

- **Regular Communication:** Stay in touch with the customer through regular communication, such as newsletters, special offers, and service reminders.
- **Loyalty Programs:** Offer loyalty programs or incentives to encourage repeat business and referrals. For example, "Join our loyalty program to receive exclusive discounts and benefits."

Service and Maintenance:

- **Service Reminders:** Send reminders for scheduled maintenance and service appointments. For example, "It's time for your vehicle's first scheduled maintenance. Please contact us to schedule an appointment."
- **Service Specials:** Offer service specials or discounts to encourage the customer to return to your dealership for maintenance and repairs. For example, "Take advantage of our special discount on oil changes this month."

Referral Programs:

- **Incentives for Referrals:** Offer incentives for customers who refer friends or family members to your dealership. For example, "Refer a friend and receive a special discount on your next service appointment."
- **Recognition:** Recognize and thank customers who provide referrals. For example, "Thank you for referring your friend to us. We appreciate your support."

Conclusion

Understanding the sales process in detail is crucial for success in the automotive industry. By mastering each stage, from prospecting and lead generation to post-sale follow-up, sales professionals can guide customers seamlessly through the journey, build lasting relationships, and achieve higher sales performance. The key to success lies in effective communication, thorough needs assessment, addressing objections, and providing exceptional customer service throughout the entire process.

Chapter 5: Building Customer Relationships

Building strong, lasting customer relationships is crucial for success in automobile sales. Customers who feel valued and understood are more likely to return for future purchases and refer others to your dealership. This chapter delves into the strategies and techniques for fostering these relationships, ensuring customer satisfaction, and turning one-time buyers into loyal advocates.

The Importance of Customer Relationships

Customer relationships are the backbone of a successful sales career. Here's why they matter:

- **Repeat Business:** Satisfied customers are more likely to return for future vehicle purchases and services.
- **Referrals:** Happy customers will refer friends, family, and colleagues, generating valuable word-of-mouth marketing.
- **Customer Loyalty:** Strong relationships

foster loyalty, reducing the likelihood of customers switching to competitors.
- **Enhanced Reputation:** A reputation for excellent customer service enhances your credibility and attracts new customers.

Building Trust and Rapport

Trust and rapport are the foundation of any successful customer relationship. Here's how to build them:

Authenticity and Transparency:

- **Be Genuine:** Authenticity is key. Customers can sense insincerity. Be yourself and show genuine interest in their needs and preferences.
- **Honesty:** Be transparent about the vehicle's features, pricing, and any potential drawbacks. Honesty builds trust and sets realistic expectations.

Active Listening:

- **Undivided Attention:** Give the customer your full attention during interactions. Avoid distractions and focus on what they are saying.
- **Empathy:** Show empathy by acknowledging their concerns and emotions. For example, "I understand that fuel efficiency is a top priority for you."

Personalized Communication:

- **Use Their Name:** Address customers by their name to make interactions more personal and engaging.
- **Tailored Recommendations:** Offer recommendations based on their specific needs and preferences. For example, "Based on your daily commute, I recommend this model for its excellent fuel economy."

Consistency:

- **Follow Through:** Follow through on promises and commitments. If you say you'll call with an update, make sure you do.
- **Reliable Service:** Consistently provide high-quality service to build reliability and trust over time.

Understanding Customer Needs

Understanding your customers' needs is essential for building strong relationships. Here's how to effectively assess their needs:

Comprehensive Needs Assessment:

- **Lifestyle Questions:** Ask about their lifestyle and how they plan to use the vehicle. For example, "Do you often go on long road trips?"

- **Family and Occupation:** Inquire about their family size and occupation to understand their space and functionality requirements. For example, "How many people do you usually travel with?"

Budget and Financing:

- **Budget Inquiry:** Discuss their budget to ensure you recommend vehicles within their price range. For example, "What's your budget for this purchase?"
- **Financing Preferences:** Ask about their financing preferences and needs. For example, "Are you looking for a lease or financing options?"

Feature Preferences:

- **Must-Have Features:** Identify the features they consider essential. For example, "What are the must-have features you're looking for in a vehicle?"
- **Technology and Safety:** Ask about their preferences for technology and safety features. For example, "Are advanced safety features important to you?"

Effective Communication Strategies

Effective communication is critical for building and maintaining customer relationships. Here are strategies to enhance your communication:

Clarity and Simplicity:

- **Avoid Jargon:** Use clear, simple language and avoid technical jargon. For example, "This feature helps you park easily" instead of "This vehicle has a park assist system."
- **Clear Explanations:** Provide clear explanations for complex features and processes. For example, "Here's how the financing process works..."

Active Listening Techniques:

- **Paraphrasing:** Repeat back what the customer has said to confirm understanding. For example, "So, you're looking for a vehicle with excellent fuel efficiency and a spacious interior, right?"
- **Clarifying Questions:** Ask clarifying questions to ensure you fully understand their needs. For example, "Can you tell me more about your daily driving routine?"

Non-Verbal Communication:

- **Body Language:** Use positive body language, such as maintaining eye contact and nodding to show engagement.
- **Facial Expressions:** Smile and use appropriate facial expressions to convey interest and friendliness.

Follow-Up Communication:

- **Timely Follow-Up:** Follow up with customers promptly after interactions to show that you value their time and business.
- **Regular Updates:** Keep customers informed about new models, promotions, and events that might interest them.

Creating a Memorable Customer Experience

Creating a memorable customer experience goes beyond just selling a car. It's about making every interaction positive and enjoyable.

Personalized Service:

- **Customized Experience:** Tailor the experience to each customer's preferences and needs. For example, if they prefer a quick process, streamline the steps for them.
- **Special Touches:** Add special touches, such as a personalized thank you note or a small gift, to make the experience memorable.

Attention to Detail:

- **Vehicle Presentation:** Ensure the vehicle is clean and well-presented when showing it to customers. A well-maintained vehicle creates a positive impression.
- **Comfort:** Make the customer comfortable

during their visit. Offer refreshments and ensure they have a pleasant waiting area.

Engaging Demonstrations:

- **Interactive Demonstrations:** Engage customers with interactive demonstrations of the vehicle's features. Let them experience the features firsthand.
- **Test Drives:** Encourage test drives to let customers experience the vehicle's performance and comfort.

Addressing Concerns Promptly:

- **Immediate Attention:** Address any concerns or issues promptly to show that you care about their satisfaction.
- **Problem Resolution:** Resolve problems quickly and effectively to maintain their trust and satisfaction.

Leveraging Technology to Enhance Relationships

Technology can be a powerful tool for enhancing customer relationships. Here's how to leverage it effectively:

Customer Relationship Management (CRM) Systems:

- **CRM Software:** Use CRM software to track customer interactions, preferences,

and purchase history. This helps you personalize future interactions.
- **Automated Follow-Ups:** Set up automated follow-up emails and reminders to stay in touch with customers.

Social Media Engagement:

- **Active Presence:** Maintain an active presence on social media platforms to engage with customers and share valuable content.
- **Respond Promptly:** Respond promptly to messages and comments to show that you value their engagement.

Personalized Email Campaigns:

- **Targeted Emails:** Send personalized emails based on customer preferences and purchase history. For example, "We thought you might be interested in our latest SUV models."
- **Exclusive Offers:** Offer exclusive promotions and discounts to loyal customers via email.

Virtual Showrooms and Online Tools:

- **Virtual Showrooms:** Use virtual showrooms to provide customers with an immersive experience from the comfort of their homes.
- **Online Configurators:** Offer online tools

that allow customers to configure and customize their vehicles before visiting the dealership.

Building Loyalty Programs

Loyalty programs can incentivize repeat business and foster long-term relationships. Here's how to create effective loyalty programs:

Rewarding Repeat Business:

- **Point Systems:** Implement a point-based system where customers earn points for purchases and services, which can be redeemed for discounts or rewards.
- **Tiered Programs:** Create tiered programs that offer increasing benefits based on the customer's level of loyalty.

Exclusive Benefits:

- **VIP Events:** Invite loyal customers to exclusive events, such as new model launches or VIP test drive events.
- **Special Discounts:** Offer special discounts on services, parts, and future vehicle purchases to loyal customers.

Referral Incentives:

- **Referral Bonuses:** Offer bonuses or discounts to customers who refer friends or family members to your dealership.

- **Recognition:** Recognize and thank customers who provide referrals with personalized notes or gifts.

Post-Sale Follow-Up and Engagement

Post-sale follow-up and engagement are crucial for maintaining customer relationships and ensuring satisfaction.

Thank You and Appreciation:

- **Personalized Thank You:** Send a personalized thank you note or email to express your appreciation for their business.
- **Follow-Up Calls:** Make a follow-up call to check in with the customer and address any questions or concerns they may have.

Feedback and Reviews:

- **Request Feedback:** Ask for feedback on their experience to show that you value their opinion. For example, "We'd love to hear your feedback on your recent purchase."
- **Encourage Reviews:** Encourage satisfied customers to leave reviews online to help build your dealership's reputation.

Service Reminders:

- **Maintenance Reminders:** Send reminders

for scheduled maintenance and service appointments to keep their vehicle in top condition.
- **Service Specials:** Offer special discounts on services to encourage customers to return to your dealership for maintenance.

Engaging Content:

- **Newsletters:** Send regular newsletters with engaging content, such as tips for vehicle maintenance, upcoming events, and new model announcements.
- **Social Media Updates:** Keep customers engaged with regular updates on social media, including promotions, events, and customer stories.

Handling Difficult Situations

Handling difficult situations effectively is essential for maintaining customer relationships. Here's how to approach these situations:

Listening and Understanding:

- **Empathetic Listening:** Listen empathetically to the customer's concerns and show that you understand their frustration.
- **Acknowledge Issues:** Acknowledge the issue and apologize for any inconvenience caused. For example, "I'm sorry to hear

about the issue with your vehicle."

Problem-Solving:

- **Identify Solutions:** Work with the customer to identify possible solutions. For example, "Let's see how we can resolve this issue for you."
- **Prompt Resolution:** Resolve the issue promptly and keep the customer informed throughout the process.

Follow-Up:

- **Confirm Satisfaction:** Follow up with the customer after resolving the issue to ensure their satisfaction. For example, "I wanted to check in and make sure everything has been resolved to your satisfaction."
- **Thank You:** Thank them for their patience and understanding. For example, "Thank you for your patience while we resolved this issue."

Continuous Improvement

Continuously improving your customer relationship skills is essential for long-term success. Here's how to focus on continuous improvement:

Ongoing Training:

- **Customer Service Training:** Participate in

ongoing customer service training to enhance your skills and stay updated on best practices.
- **Product Knowledge:** Continuously improve your product knowledge to provide accurate and helpful information to customers.

Self-Reflection:

- **Reflect on Interactions:** Regularly reflect on your interactions with customers to identify areas for improvement. For example, "How could I have handled that situation better?"
- **Seek Feedback:** Ask colleagues and managers for feedback on your performance to gain new perspectives.

Staying Informed:

- **Industry Trends:** Stay informed about industry trends and changes to better understand customer needs and preferences.
- **Customer Insights:** Pay attention to customer insights and feedback to identify emerging trends and preferences.

Conclusion

Building strong customer relationships in the automotive industry requires a combination of authenticity, effective communication, personalized service, and continuous improvement. By understanding customer needs, providing exceptional service, and leveraging technology, sales professionals can create lasting relationships that drive repeat business, referrals, and long-term success. The key is to focus on creating memorable experiences, addressing concerns promptly, and continuously enhancing your skills to meet and exceed customer expectations.

Chapter 6: Handling Objections in Automotive Sales

Handling objections is a critical skill for automotive sales professionals. Objections are natural in the sales process and often indicate a customer's concerns or hesitations. Mastering the art of addressing objections effectively can significantly increase your closing ratio and customer satisfaction. This chapter explores various types of objections, strategies for handling them, and tips to turn objections into opportunities.

Understanding Types of Objections

Objections in car sales can vary widely, but they generally fall into several categories. Each objection type requires a tailored approach for resolution. Here are common types of objections:

1. **Price Objections:**

- Customers may express concerns about the vehicle's price being too high or not aligning with their budget.
- Example: "I think this car is out of my price range."

2. **Feature Objections:**

    - Customers may focus on specific features they desire or lack in the vehicle.
    - Example: "I was hoping for a vehicle with a sunroof."

3. **Timing Objections:**

    - Customers may hesitate due to timing issues, such as not being ready to make a purchase immediately.
    - Example: "I need more time to think about it."

4. **Trust Objections:**

    - Customers may have doubts about the dealership's reputation, vehicle reliability, or the salesperson's honesty.
    - Example: "I'm not sure about the reliability of this brand."

5. **Comparison Objections:**

    - Customers may compare your offer with competitors or alternative

options.
- Example: "I've seen similar models at another dealership for a lower price."

6. **Need-Satisfaction Objections:**
   - Customers may not see how the vehicle meets their specific needs or preferences.
   - Example: "I'm concerned about the fuel efficiency of this model."

7. **Authority Objections:**
   - Customers may need to consult with someone else (e.g., spouse, family member) before making a decision.
   - Example: "I need to discuss this with my spouse before moving forward."

Strategies for Handling Objections

Effective objection handling involves active listening, empathy, and providing relevant information to address customer concerns. Here are strategies to handle objections effectively:

1. Active Listening and Empathy:
   - **Listen Fully:** Allow customers to express their objections fully without interruption.
   - **Empathize:** Show understanding of their concerns and acknowledge their

perspective.

2. Clarify and Confirm:

- **Clarify the Objection:** Repeat back the objection to ensure you understand it correctly.
- **Confirm Understanding:** Ask clarifying questions to get to the root of the objection. For example, "Could you tell me more about your concerns regarding the price?"

3. Provide Relevant Information:

- **Highlight Benefits:** Emphasize the value and benefits of the vehicle to justify the price or features. For example, "This model includes advanced safety features that are crucial for your family's safety."
- **Address Concerns:** Provide specific information or data to address their objections. For example, "The fuel efficiency of this model is higher than similar vehicles in its class."

4. Use Stories and Examples:

- **Case Studies:** Share success stories or case studies of other customers who had similar objections but found satisfaction with their purchase.
- **Demonstrations:** Offer demonstrations or test drives to showcase the vehicle's features and performance.

5. Overcome with Value:

- **Value Justification:** Articulate the overall value proposition of the vehicle and dealership services. For example, "Considering the safety features, warranty, and reliability, this vehicle offers great value for its price."

6. Handle Price Objections:

- **Cost-Value Comparison:** Compare the vehicle's cost with its long-term value and benefits. For example, "While the initial cost may seem high, this model has lower maintenance costs and higher resale value."

7. Address Feature Objections:

- **Alternative Features:** Offer alternative models or packages that better align with their desired features. For example, "If a sunroof is important to you, we have another model that includes this feature."

8. Timing Objections:

- **Urgency and Benefits:** Highlight time-sensitive promotions or benefits of purchasing now, such as limited-time financing offers or vehicle availability. For example, "If you decide today, we can offer special financing options that expire soon."

9. Build Trust:

- **Establish Credibility:** Share testimonials or reviews from satisfied customers to build trust in the dealership and brand.
- **Transparency:** Be honest and transparent about the vehicle's history, condition, and any additional costs.

10. Handle Comparison Objections:

- **Unique Selling Points:** Highlight the unique features or benefits that set your dealership or vehicles apart from competitors. For example, "Our dealership offers a comprehensive warranty and exceptional customer service that you won't find elsewhere."

11. Need-Satisfaction Objections:

- **Customization Options:** Discuss customization options or aftermarket accessories to meet their specific needs. For example, "We can add a roof rack to this model to accommodate your outdoor gear."

12. Authority Objections:

- **Involve Decision-Makers:** Offer to include their spouse or family member in the discussion or decision-making process. Provide information that helps them make an informed decision.

Real-Life Examples and Case Studies

Real-life examples and case studies can illustrate effective objection handling techniques in action:

Example 1: Addressing Price Objection

- *Objection:* "I think this car is out of my price range."
- *Response:* "I understand your concern. Many customers initially feel that way. Let me show you the long-term cost savings and benefits this vehicle offers compared to others in its class."

Example 2: Handling Feature Objection

- *Objection:* "I was hoping for a vehicle with a sunroof."
- *Response:* "I appreciate your preference for a sunroof. While this model doesn't have one, we have another model with a panoramic sunroof that might interest you."

Example 3: Overcoming Timing Objection

- *Objection:* "I need more time to think about it."
- *Response:* "I understand it's an important decision. However, I want to ensure you don't miss out on our current promotion that ends this week. Let's discuss how we can make this decision easier for you."

Case Study: Turning Trust Objection into

Opportunity

- *Objection:* "I'm not sure about the reliability of this brand."
- *Strategy:* Provide data on the brand's reliability ratings and share testimonials from long-time customers who have had positive experiences with the brand.

Additional Tips for Mastering Objection Handling

1. Preparation:

- **Know Your Products:** Have in-depth knowledge of the vehicles you sell, including features, specifications, and competitive advantages.
- **Anticipate Objections:** Based on common objections, prepare responses and counter-arguments in advance.

2. Practice Active Listening:

- **Empathetic Listening:** Focus on understanding the customer's concerns and motivations behind their objections.

3. Role-Playing:

- **Team Exercises:** Conduct role-playing exercises with colleagues to practice handling objections in various scenarios.
- **Feedback:** Provide and receive feedback to

improve objection handling skills.

4. Continuous Learning:

- **Attend Training:** Participate in workshops, seminars, and online courses to enhance objection handling techniques and sales skills.
- **Industry Updates:** Stay informed about industry trends, customer preferences, and competitor offerings.

5. Use Technology:

- **CRM Systems:** Utilize CRM systems to track customer objections, responses, and outcomes for continuous improvement.
- **Digital Tools:** Use digital tools for virtual demonstrations, online vehicle tours, and personalized follow-up communications.

6. Maintain Positivity:

- **Positive Attitude:** Approach objections as opportunities to provide solutions and build rapport with customers.
- **Persistence:** Don't give up after the first objection. Stay persistent and focused on finding a mutually beneficial solution.

Conclusion

Mastering the art of handling objections is essential for automotive sales professionals to build trust, overcome customer hesitations, and ultimately close more sales. By understanding the types of objections, employing effective strategies, using real-life examples, and continuously refining your skills, you can turn objections into opportunities to strengthen customer relationships and achieve sales success. Remember, objection handling is not just about persuasion but about understanding and addressing customer needs to create a positive buying experience.

Chapter 7: Closing the Sale in Automotive Sales

Closing the sale is the culmination of the sales process in automotive sales. It involves guiding the customer towards a purchasing decision and securing their commitment. This chapter explores effective closing techniques, negotiation strategies, steps to finalize paperwork, handling objections during the closing phase, and the crucial follow-up process to ensure customer satisfaction.

Effective Closing Techniques

Closing techniques are methods used to encourage the customer to make a purchasing decision. Different techniques can be applied depending on the customer's preferences and readiness to buy.

1. Assumptive Close:

- **Definition:** Assume the customer is ready to buy and proceed with the next steps.

- **Example:** "Let's finalize the paperwork so you can drive your new car home today."

2. Summary Close:

- **Definition:** Summarize the key benefits and features to reinforce the value of the vehicle.
- **Example:** "To recap, this car offers exceptional fuel efficiency, advanced safety features, and a luxurious interior."

3. Direct Close:

- **Definition:** Ask directly for the sale in a confident manner.
- **Example:** "Are you ready to move forward with the purchase of this vehicle today?"

4. Choice Close:

- **Definition:** Offer the customer a choice between two options, both leading to a sale.
- **Example:** "Would you prefer the silver model with leather seats, or the black model with the upgraded sound system?"

5. Time-Limited Close:

- **Definition:** Create urgency by highlighting time-sensitive offers or promotions.
- **Example:** "Our current financing offer ends this weekend. If you decide now, you can take advantage of these special terms."

6. Trial Close:

- **Definition:** Gauge the customer's readiness to buy by asking trial questions.
- **Example:** "If we can agree on the financing terms, would you be prepared to sign the paperwork today?"

Negotiation Strategies

Negotiation is a crucial part of the closing process, especially when discussing price, financing terms, or additional features. Effective negotiation strategies can lead to a mutually beneficial agreement.

1. Understanding Customer Needs:

- **Strategy:** Focus on understanding the customer's priorities and preferences.
- **Example:** "Based on your budget and requirements, let's find a solution that meets your needs."

2. Flexibility:

- **Strategy:** Be flexible and willing to adjust terms to reach an agreement.
- **Example:** "We can offer a lower price if you're able to finalize the purchase today."

3. Highlighting Value:

- **Strategy:** Emphasize the value proposition of the vehicle and dealership services.

- **Example:** "Considering the warranty and complimentary maintenance, this offer provides great value."

4. Multiple Options:

- **Strategy:** Offer multiple packages or financing options to provide choices.
- **Example:** "Here are three different financing plans. Let's find the one that fits your budget."

5. Win-Win Solutions:

- **Strategy:** Aim for a solution where both parties feel they've gained something of value.
- **Example:** "Let's work together to find terms that are fair and beneficial for both sides."

Steps in Finalizing Paperwork

Finalizing paperwork involves completing necessary documentation to formalize the purchase agreement, financing terms, and any trade-in details. It's essential to ensure accuracy and clarity throughout this process.

1. Purchase Agreement:

- **Definition:** Document outlining the terms of the vehicle sale, including price, specifications, and warranties.

- **Steps:** Review the agreement with the customer to ensure all details are accurate and understood.

2. Financing Documents:

- **Definition:** Contracts outlining the terms of the loan or lease agreement.
- **Steps:** Explain the financing terms clearly and answer any questions the customer may have.

3. Trade-In Paperwork:

- **Definition:** Documentation related to the trade-in vehicle, including ownership transfer and valuation.
- **Steps:** Discuss the trade-in value and finalize the necessary paperwork.

4. Legal Compliance:

- **Definition:** Ensure compliance with legal requirements and regulations governing vehicle sales.
- **Steps:** Verify that all paperwork meets legal standards and obtain necessary signatures.

Handling Objections During the Closing Process

Objections may arise during the closing process, requiring careful handling to address customer concerns and maintain momentum towards a sale.

1. Price Objections:

- **Response:** Highlight the value and benefits of the vehicle to justify the price.
- **Example:** "Considering the long-term savings on fuel and maintenance, this vehicle offers excellent value."

2. Timing Objections:

- **Response:** Create urgency by emphasizing time-sensitive offers or limited availability.
- **Example:** "This model is in high demand, and our current inventory is selling quickly. If you decide now, you can secure this vehicle."

3. Feature Objections:

- **Response:** Discuss alternative models or packages that better meet the customer's preferences.
- **Example:** "If a sunroof is important to you, we have another model with a panoramic sunroof available."

4. Trust Objections:

- **Response:** Provide reassurance through testimonials, reviews, or warranty information.
- **Example:** "Many of our customers have praised the reliability and durability of this

brand. Let me show you some customer testimonials."

Tips for Overcoming Buyer Hesitation

Buyer hesitation is common and can be overcome with proactive strategies that build confidence and trust in the purchase decision.

1. Build Rapport:

- **Strategy:** Strengthen the relationship by demonstrating empathy and understanding.
- **Example:** "I understand this is a significant decision. Let's address any concerns you have before moving forward."

2. Provide Assurance:

- **Strategy:** Reassure the customer through factual information and transparent communication.
- **Example:** "Our dealership has a reputation for exceptional customer service and support. We'll be here to assist you every step of the way."

3. Offer Value-Added Services:

- **Strategy:** Highlight additional services such as extended warranties or maintenance packages.
- **Example:** "With our extended warranty, you'll have peace of mind knowing your

vehicle is covered for years to come."

4. Demonstrate Confidence:

- **Strategy:** Project confidence in the product and dealership services.
- **Example:** "I'm confident that this vehicle meets all your requirements and exceeds your expectations in terms of performance and reliability."

The Importance of Follow-Up

Post-sale follow-up is crucial for ensuring customer satisfaction, addressing any post-purchase concerns, and fostering long-term relationships.

1. Thank You and Appreciation:

- **Action:** Send a personalized thank you note or email to express appreciation for the customer's business.
- **Example:** "Thank you for choosing [Dealership Name]. We appreciate your trust and look forward to serving you in the future."

2. Follow-Up Calls:

- **Action:** Make a follow-up call to check in with the customer and address any questions or issues.
- **Example:** "I wanted to see how you're

enjoying your new car and if there's anything else I can assist you with."

3. Addressing Concerns Promptly:

- **Action:** Respond promptly to any concerns or issues that arise after the sale.
- **Example:** "If you experience any issues or have questions about your vehicle, please don't hesitate to reach out to us."

4. Building Long-Term Relationships:

- **Action:** Maintain regular communication through newsletters, special offers, and service reminders.
- **Example:** "Stay updated on our latest promotions and events by subscribing to our monthly newsletter."

Conclusion

Closing the sale in automotive sales requires skill, confidence, and a customer-centric approach. By mastering effective closing techniques, negotiating with transparency and flexibility, finalizing paperwork accurately, addressing objections proactively, overcoming buyer hesitation, and conducting thorough follow-up, sales professionals can create positive buying experiences that lead to long-term customer satisfaction and loyalty. Remember, each interaction is an opportunity to build trust and showcase the value of your dealership and the vehicles you sell.

Chapter 8: Building Long-Term Customer Relationships in Automotive Sales

Building long-term customer relationships is essential for sustained success in automotive sales. This chapter explores strategies, techniques, and principles to foster meaningful connections with customers, enhance satisfaction, and cultivate loyalty over time.

Importance of Customer Retention

Customer retention refers to the ability to keep customers coming back to your dealership for future purchases and services. It is significantly more cost-effective to retain existing customers than to acquire new ones. Here's why customer retention matters:

1. **Financial Impact:** Repeat customers tend to spend more and are more likely to purchase additional services or upgrades.//
2. **Referrals and Word-of-Mouth:** Satisfied customers are more likely to refer friends and family, contributing to new business growth.

3. **Brand Advocacy:** Loyal customers become advocates for your dealership, promoting your services through positive reviews and testimonials.

Personalized Customer Service Approaches

Personalization enhances the customer experience by tailoring interactions to meet individual preferences and needs. Effective personalized service approaches include:

- **Customer Profiling:** Collect and use data to understand customer preferences, purchase history, and communication preferences.

- **Customized Communication:** Personalize communication channels such as emails, phone calls, and in-person interactions based on customer preferences.

- **Tailored Recommendations:** Offer personalized vehicle recommendations, service packages, and promotions that align with the customer's interests.

Effective Communication Methods

Clear and effective communication is fundamental to building strong customer relationships. Key communication methods include:

- **Active Listening:** Listen attentively to understand customer concerns, preferences, and expectations.
- **Clear and Transparent Information:** Provide accurate and transparent information about vehicles, pricing, financing options, and services.
- **Timely Follow-Up:** Follow up promptly after sales and service interactions to ensure customer satisfaction and address any concerns.

Leveraging Technology for Relationship Management

Technology plays a crucial role in managing and nurturing customer relationships. Effective use of technology includes:

- **Customer Relationship Management (CRM) Systems:** Use CRM systems to track customer interactions, preferences, and purchase history.
- **Automated Communication:** Implement automated email campaigns, personalized messages, and reminders for service appointments or vehicle updates.
- **Digital Tools and Platforms:** Utilize digital platforms for virtual vehicle tours, online service scheduling, and customer

feedback collection.

Maintaining Customer Loyalty Programs

Loyalty programs incentivize repeat business and reward customer loyalty. Components of successful loyalty programs include:

- **Rewards and Incentives:** Offer discounts on future purchases, free services, or exclusive access to events for loyal customers.

- **Tiered Benefits:** Provide tiered membership levels based on customer spending or engagement, offering increasing benefits at higher levels.

- **Personalized Rewards:** Tailor rewards and incentives based on individual customer preferences and purchase behaviors.

Handling Customer Feedback

Feedback from customers provides valuable insights for improving products and services. Strategies for handling customer feedback include:

- **Active Listening:** Acknowledge and appreciate customer feedback, whether positive or negative.

- **Response and Resolution:** Respond promptly to customer concerns, take ownership of issues, and provide solutions to resolve problems.

- **Continuous Improvement:** Use feedback to identify areas for improvement in products, services, and customer experiences.

Resolving Issues to Enhance Satisfaction

Effective issue resolution is critical for maintaining customer satisfaction and loyalty. Steps for resolving customer issues include:

- **Empathy and Understanding:** Listen to the customer's concerns with empathy and understanding.
- **Timely Response:** Address issues promptly and communicate realistic timelines for resolution.
- **Follow-Up:** Follow up with the customer to ensure the issue has been resolved satisfactorily and offer additional support if needed.

Building Trust and Credibility

Trust is the foundation of long-term customer relationships. Strategies for building trust include:

- **Consistency:** Consistently deliver high-quality products and services that meet or exceed customer expectations.

- **Transparency:** Be transparent in pricing, policies, and communication with customers.
- **Integrity:** Uphold ethical standards and integrity in all interactions with customers and stakeholders.

Cultivating Emotional Connections

Emotional connections foster strong customer loyalty and advocacy. Ways to cultivate emotional connections include:

- **Personalized Interactions:** Remember and acknowledge important milestones or preferences of individual customers.
- **Creating Memorable Experiences:** Go beyond expectations to create memorable experiences during sales, service, and post-purchase interactions.
- **Expressing Gratitude:** Show appreciation for customer loyalty through personalized thank-you notes, special offers, or exclusive invitations.

Continuous Improvement in Customer Relationships

Continuous improvement is essential for adapting

to changing customer expectations and market dynamics. Strategies for continuous improvement include:

- **Feedback Loops:** Implement mechanisms to gather ongoing feedback from customers about their experiences.

- **Training and Development:** Invest in training programs to enhance employee skills in customer service, communication, and relationship-building.

- **Market Research:** Stay informed about industry trends, competitor offerings, and customer preferences to anticipate and respond to changes effectively.

Conclusion

Building long-term customer relationships in automotive sales requires dedication, strategy, and a customer-centric approach. By prioritizing customer retention, delivering personalized service, leveraging technology effectively, maintaining loyalty programs, handling feedback constructively, resolving issues promptly, building trust, cultivating emotional connections, and continuously improving customer relationships, dealerships can create lasting value and loyalty. Remember, each customer interaction is an opportunity to strengthen relationships, exceed expectations, and build a reputation for excellence in customer service within the automotive industry.

Chapter 9: Effective Sales Presentation Techniques in Automotive Sales

Delivering effective sales presentations is crucial for engaging customers, showcasing vehicle features, and guiding them towards a purchasing decision. This chapter explores proven techniques, strategies, and best practices to create impactful sales presentations in the automotive industry.

Importance of Effective Sales Presentations

Effective sales presentations serve multiple purposes in automotive sales:

- **Engagement:** Capture and maintain customer interest throughout the presentation.
- **Education:** Inform customers about vehicle features, benefits, and options.
- **Persuasion:** Influence customer perceptions and decisions towards making a purchase.
- **Differentiation:** Highlight unique selling points and competitive advantages of your dealership and vehicles.

Steps for Preparing Sales Presentations

Preparation is key to delivering a polished and persuasive sales presentation. Steps for preparing effective sales presentations include:

1. **Research and Planning:**
   - **Know Your Audience:** Understand the preferences, needs, and expectations of your prospective customers.
   - **Research Vehicles:** Familiarize yourself with the features, specifications, and benefits of the vehicles you'll present.
2. **Set Objectives:**
   - **Define Goals:** Clarify the specific objectives of the presentation, such as demonstrating key features or addressing customer concerns.
3. **Craft a Storyline:**
   - **Create Structure:** Develop a logical flow for your presentation, starting from introduction to vehicle demonstration and closing.
4. **Gather Materials:**
   - **Visual Aids:** Prepare visual aids such as brochures, spec sheets, and multimedia presentations to support your talk.

Understanding Customer Needs

Tailor your presentation to address the unique needs, preferences, and concerns of each customer. Techniques for understanding customer needs include:

- **Active Listening:** Listen attentively to customer questions, comments, and preferences.
- **Ask Probing Questions:** Clarify customer priorities and expectations to customize your presentation accordingly.
- **Adaptability:** Be prepared to adjust your presentation based on customer feedback and reactions.

Demonstrating Vehicle Features Effectively

Effectively demonstrating vehicle features involves showcasing their functionality, benefits, and relevance to customer needs. Techniques for demonstrating vehicle features include:

- **Hands-On Approach:** Encourage customers to interact with the vehicle and experience its features firsthand.
- **Highlight Benefits:** Emphasize how specific features address customer concerns or preferences (e.g., safety, comfort, technology).
- **Customization:** Demonstrate customizable

features or optional packages that align with customer preferences.

Storytelling Techniques

Storytelling can make your presentation more engaging and memorable. Techniques for incorporating storytelling into your presentation include:

- **Use Case Scenarios:** Share real-life stories or testimonials from satisfied customers who benefited from specific vehicle features.
- **Paint a Picture:** Describe how owning the vehicle can enhance the customer's lifestyle or address their specific needs.
- **Create Emotional Appeal:** Appeal to customer emotions by highlighting the positive experiences and outcomes associated with the vehicle.

Handling Objections During Presentations

Anticipate and address objections that may arise during your presentation. Techniques for handling objections include:

- **Active Listening:** Fully understand the objection before responding.
- **Provide Solutions:** Offer solutions or alternatives that address the customer's

concerns.
- **Reinforce Benefits:** Emphasize the overall value and benefits of the vehicle to justify the price or address specific objections.

Utilizing Visual Aids and Technology

Visual aids and technology can enhance the effectiveness of your presentation by making information more accessible and engaging. Techniques for using visual aids and technology include:

- **Interactive Presentations:** Use multimedia tools, such as videos or interactive demos, to demonstrate vehicle features and benefits.
- **Virtual Tours:** Offer virtual tours or 360-degree views of vehicles to provide a comprehensive understanding of their design and functionality.
- **Digital Brochures:** Share digital brochures or spec sheets that customers can review during or after the presentation.

Adapting Presentations to Different Customer Types

Tailor your presentation style and content to match the preferences and communication styles of different customer types. Techniques for adapting presentations include:

- **Analytical Customers:** Provide detailed technical information and data about vehicle specifications and performance.
- **Social Customers:** Engage in conversations, share stories, and focus on how the vehicle fits into their social and lifestyle needs.
- **Assertive Customers:** Be direct and confident in presenting key features and benefits, and be prepared to address challenges or objections.

Evaluating Presentation Effectiveness

Assessing the effectiveness of your sales presentations helps identify strengths, areas for improvement, and opportunities for enhancing customer engagement. Techniques for evaluating presentation effectiveness include:

- **Feedback Surveys:** Collect feedback from customers regarding their experience and satisfaction with the presentation.
- **Self-Assessment:** Reflect on your performance and identify areas where adjustments or improvements can be made.
- **Performance Metrics:** Track metrics such as conversion rates, customer retention, and feedback scores to measure presentation impact.

Conclusion

Mastering effective sales presentation techniques is essential for automotive sales professionals to engage customers, showcase vehicle features persuasively, and guide them towards making informed purchasing decisions. By preparing thoroughly, understanding customer needs, demonstrating vehicle features effectively, incorporating storytelling techniques, handling objections proactively, leveraging visual aids and technology, adapting to different customer types, and evaluating presentation effectiveness, sales professionals can create compelling presentations that leave a lasting impression and drive sales success. Remember, each presentation is an opportunity to build trust, demonstrate expertise, and create a positive buying experience for customers in the competitive automotive market.

Chapter 10: Effective Customer Communication Strategies in Automotive Sales

Effective customer communication is fundamental to success in automotive sales. This chapter explores proven strategies, techniques, and best practices for communicating effectively with customers to build relationships, understand needs, address concerns, and guide them through the sales process.

Building Rapport

Building rapport establishes trust and fosters positive relationships with customers. Techniques for building rapport include:

- **Greeting and Introduction:** Make a warm and friendly initial greeting to create a welcoming atmosphere.

- **Active Listening:** Pay attention to the customer's words, tone, and body language to demonstrate genuine interest.

- **Find Common Ground:** Establish common interests or shared experiences to create a connection with the customer.

Active Listening Techniques

Active listening involves fully concentrating, understanding, responding thoughtfully, and remembering what is said. Techniques for active listening include:

- **Maintain Eye Contact:** Demonstrate attentiveness and interest by maintaining eye contact with the customer.

- **Paraphrasing:** Repeat or summarize what the customer has said to confirm understanding and show empathy.

- **Ask Clarifying Questions:** Seek clarification to ensure you grasp the customer's concerns or preferences accurately.

Effective Questioning Skills

Effective questioning helps uncover customer needs, preferences, and priorities. Types of effective questions include:

- **Open-Ended Questions:** Encourage customers to elaborate and provide detailed information.
- **Closed-Ended Questions:** Seek specific information or confirm details with brief answers.
- **Probing Questions:** Explore deeper into customer motivations, concerns, or preferences.

Adapting Communication Styles

Adapting your communication style enhances effectiveness and rapport with different customers. Styles to consider include:

- **Assertive Communication:** Clearly express thoughts, needs, and expectations while respecting customer preferences.

- **Collaborative Communication:** Work together with the customer to find solutions or make decisions.

- **Empathetic Communication:** Show understanding and sensitivity towards customer concerns or emotions.

Handling Difficult Conversations

Difficult conversations may arise during negotiations, objections, or addressing customer concerns. Strategies for handling difficult conversations include:

- **Stay Calm and Professional:** Maintain composure and focus on resolving the issue constructively.

- **Active Listening:** Validate the customer's concerns and demonstrate empathy before providing solutions.

- **Offer Solutions:** Propose alternatives or compromises that address the customer's concerns effectively.

Utilizing Virtual Communication Tools

Virtual communication tools facilitate remote interactions and enhance customer engagement. Tools to consider include:

- **Video Conferencing:** Conduct virtual

meetings, vehicle tours, or demonstrations via video calls.

- **Online Chat:** Provide instant support, answer questions, and assist customers via live chat on your dealership website.
- **Virtual Reality (VR) Tours:** Offer immersive experiences of vehicles through VR technology for remote customers.

Cross-Cultural Communication Considerations

Cross-cultural communication requires sensitivity and understanding of cultural differences. Considerations include:

- **Respect Cultural Norms:** Be aware of cultural differences in communication styles, gestures, and etiquette.
- **Avoid Assumptions:** Seek clarification and adapt your approach to respect and accommodate diverse cultural backgrounds.
- **Build Trust:** Foster trust and rapport by demonstrating cultural awareness and respect for differences.

Strategies for Enhancing Communication Effectiveness

Strategies to enhance communication effectiveness in automotive sales include:

- **Clear and Concise Communication:** Use language that is easy to understand and avoids jargon or technical terms unless necessary.

- **Follow-Up Communication:** Maintain regular contact with customers through follow-up calls, emails, or newsletters to nurture relationships.

- **Feedback Loop:** Solicit feedback from customers to assess satisfaction levels and identify areas for improvement.

- **Training and Development:** Invest in ongoing training to enhance communication skills, product knowledge, and customer service excellence.

Conclusion

Effective customer communication is essential for building relationships, understanding customer needs, and guiding them through the automotive sales process. By mastering techniques such as building rapport, active listening, effective questioning, adapting communication styles, handling difficult conversations, utilizing virtual communication tools, considering cross-cultural differences, and implementing strategies to enhance communication effectiveness, sales professionals can create positive experiences and drive success in automotive sales. Remember, every interaction is an opportunity to build trust, demonstrate expertise, and exceed customer expectations in the competitive automotive market.

Chapter 11: Negotiation Strategies in Automotive Sales

Negotiation is a critical skill in automotive sales that involves reaching mutually beneficial agreements with customers. This chapter explores comprehensive strategies, techniques, and principles to negotiate effectively and ethically in the automotive industry.

Understanding Negotiation Principles

Negotiation principles form the foundation for successful outcomes in automotive sales:

- **Preparation:** Research customer preferences, market trends, and competitive offers before negotiations.
- **Communication:** Clearly convey your dealership's value proposition, pricing rationale, and willingness to accommodate customer needs.
- **Flexibility:** Remain adaptable and open to

creative solutions that meet both parties' interests.

Advanced Negotiation Techniques

Advanced negotiation techniques enhance your ability to navigate complex negotiations effectively:

- **BATNA (Best Alternative to a Negotiated Agreement):** Identify your fallback options and leverage them to strengthen your position.
- **Anchoring:** Set a favorable starting point (e.g., price or terms) to influence customer perceptions and expectations.
- **Exploring Interests:** Understand underlying motivations and priorities to propose solutions that align with customer interests.

Psychological Aspects of Negotiation

Understanding psychological dynamics can influence negotiation outcomes positively:

- **Empathy:** Demonstrate empathy to build rapport and understand the customer's perspective.
- **Emotional Intelligence:** Manage your emotions and recognize emotional cues

from the customer during negotiations.

- **Reciprocity:** Offer concessions or benefits to encourage reciprocal behavior from the customer.

Handling Objections During Negotiations

Effectively addressing objections is crucial for progressing towards a successful agreement:

- **Active Listening:** Listen attentively to objections to understand their root causes and concerns.
- **Clarification:** Ask probing questions to clarify objections and gather additional information.
- **Reframing:** Reframe objections as opportunities for mutual problem-solving and agreement.

Creating Win-Win Outcomes

Strive for win-win outcomes that satisfy both the dealership's objectives and customer needs:

- **Value Creation:** Identify and communicate additional value in terms of features, services, or financing options.
- **Trade-Offs:** Prioritize negotiation points and be prepared to make concessions on

less critical issues.

- **Long-Term Relationships:** Emphasize building a long-term relationship based on trust and mutual benefit.

Understanding Buyer Motivations

Understanding buyer motivations helps tailor negotiations to meet customer expectations:

- **Financial Considerations:** Recognize budget constraints and affordability concerns influencing purchase decisions.

- **Emotional Drivers:** Address emotional factors such as status, comfort, safety, and lifestyle preferences.

- **Decision-Making Process:** Adapt negotiation strategies based on whether the buyer is making an emotional or rational decision.

Leveraging Power Dynamics

Awareness of power dynamics can influence negotiation strategies and outcomes:

- **Information Advantage:** Utilize comprehensive product knowledge and market insights to convey credibility.

- **Timing:** Capitalize on favorable market

conditions, promotions, or limited-time offers to create urgency.

- **Authority:** Ensure alignment with decision-makers who have authority to finalize agreements.

Ethical Considerations in Negotiation

Maintain ethical standards throughout the negotiation process:

- **Transparency:** Provide accurate information and disclose relevant terms and conditions.
- **Fairness:** Ensure fairness in pricing, incentives, and negotiation practices with all customers.
- **Integrity:** Uphold dealership policies and ethical guidelines in all negotiations and customer interactions.

Strategies for Negotiating Effectively

Strategies to enhance negotiation effectiveness in automotive sales include:

- **Preparation and Planning:** Anticipate potential challenges and prepare strategies to address them proactively.
- **Active Engagement:** Maintain active

engagement throughout negotiations, demonstrating commitment to reaching a mutually beneficial agreement.

- **Closing Techniques:** Apply effective closing techniques to finalize agreements once negotiation terms are agreed upon.

Conclusion

Mastering negotiation strategies is essential for achieving successful outcomes in automotive sales negotiations. By understanding negotiation principles, employing advanced techniques, recognizing psychological dynamics, handling objections effectively, creating win-win outcomes, understanding buyer motivations, leveraging power dynamics ethically, and implementing strategies for effective negotiation, sales professionals can build trust, establish long-term customer relationships, and drive business growth. Remember, each negotiation presents an opportunity to showcase professionalism, expertise, and commitment to customer satisfaction in the competitive automotive market.

Chapter 12: Closing Techniques and Strategies in Automotive Sales

Closing the sale is the culmination of effective communication, negotiation, and persuasion in automotive sales. This chapter explores comprehensive techniques, strategies, and best practices to successfully close deals and achieve customer commitments.

Understanding the Importance of Closing

Closing is the final step in the sales process where a customer makes a purchasing decision. Key aspects of closing include:

- **Commitment:** Obtain customer commitment to finalize the purchase or move forward with the transaction.

- **Revenue Generation:** Generate revenue for the dealership through vehicle sales, service packages, or add-on options.

- **Customer Satisfaction:** Ensure customer satisfaction by addressing concerns and providing solutions.

Techniques for Overcoming Objections

Effective objection-handling techniques facilitate smoother closing processes:

- **Anticipate Objections:** Identify potential

objections and prepare responses to address them proactively.

- **Listen Actively:** Acknowledge customer concerns and demonstrate understanding before providing solutions.
- **Reframe Objections:** Turn objections into opportunities to highlight the value and benefits of the purchase.

Psychological Aspects of Closing

Understanding psychological dynamics enhances closing effectiveness:

- **Sense of Ownership:** Encourage customers to visualize ownership and imagine themselves enjoying the benefits of the vehicle.
- **Urgency and Scarcity:** Create urgency through limited-time offers, promotions, or vehicle availability to prompt immediate action.
- **Decision Fatigue:** Simplify choices and guide customers towards making a confident decision without overwhelming them.

Building Urgency

Creating a sense of urgency motivates customers

to take action promptly:

- **Limited-Time Offers:** Highlight special promotions, discounts, or incentives available for a limited period.

- **Inventory Status:** Communicate availability and scarcity of popular models or configurations to encourage timely decisions.

- **Customer-Specific Benefits:** Offer personalized benefits or additional incentives for immediate purchases.

Trial Closes

Trial closes gauge customer readiness and pave the way for final commitment:

- **Assumptive Close:** Assume the sale by asking questions that imply the customer's readiness to proceed (e.g., "Would you prefer morning or afternoon delivery?").

- **Alternative Choice Close:** Offer two favorable options to guide the customer towards a decision (e.g., "Would you prefer the blue model or the silver model?").

- **Summary Close:** Summarize key benefits and features discussed to reinforce the customer's decision-making process.

Handling Buyer Hesitations

Addressing buyer hesitations builds confidence and resolves lingering concerns:

- **Clarify Benefits:** Reinforce the value and benefits of the vehicle to reassure customers of their decision.

- **Provide Social Proof:** Share testimonials or success stories from satisfied customers who made similar purchases.

- **Offer Guarantees:** Provide assurances such as satisfaction guarantees, warranty coverage, or return policies to alleviate concerns.

Closing Effectively in Different Sales Scenarios

Adapting closing techniques to various sales scenarios enhances success rates:

- **First-Time Buyers:** Guide first-time buyers through the process with clear explanations and patient guidance.

- **Repeat Customers:** Acknowledge loyalty and offer personalized incentives to encourage repeat purchases.

- **Fleet Sales:** Highlight bulk purchase benefits, cost savings, and customization options tailored to fleet needs.

Measuring Closing Effectiveness

Assessing closing effectiveness provides insights for continuous improvement:

- **Conversion Rates:** Track the percentage of leads or prospects who convert into paying customers.

- **Sales Metrics:** Analyze sales performance indicators such as average deal size, sales cycle length, and closing ratios.

- **Customer Feedback:** Solicit feedback from customers regarding their purchasing experience and satisfaction levels.

Strategies for Continuous Improvement

Strategies to enhance closing effectiveness and achieve sales goals include:

- **Role-Playing Exercises:** Practice different closing techniques and scenarios with colleagues to refine skills and build confidence.

- **Feedback and Coaching:** Seek feedback from managers or mentors to identify strengths and areas for improvement.

- **Training and Development:** Participate in ongoing training programs to stay updated on industry trends, product knowledge, and sales techniques.

Conclusion

Mastering closing techniques is essential for achieving successful outcomes in automotive sales. By understanding the importance of closing, employing effective objection-handling techniques, leveraging psychological aspects, creating urgency, using trial closes, addressing buyer hesitations, adapting to different sales scenarios, measuring closing effectiveness, and implementing strategies for continuous improvement, sales professionals can enhance customer satisfaction, drive revenue, and build long-term success in the competitive automotive market. Remember, each closing opportunity is a chance to demonstrate professionalism, build trust, and deliver exceptional customer service.

Chapter 13: Customer Service Excellence in Automotive Sales

Customer service excellence is crucial for building lasting relationships, fostering loyalty, and driving satisfaction in automotive sales. This chapter explores comprehensive strategies, techniques, and best practices to deliver exceptional customer service that exceeds expectations.

Creating a Customer-Centric Culture

A customer-centric culture prioritizes customer needs and satisfaction throughout the dealership:

- **Leadership Commitment:** Demonstrate leadership commitment to customer service excellence through actions and policies.

- **Employee Engagement:** Involve employees in decision-making processes and encourage them to prioritize customer satisfaction.

- **Continuous Feedback:** Solicit feedback from customers and employees to identify areas for improvement and celebrate successes.

Effective Communication with Customers

Clear and effective communication enhances customer interactions and satisfaction:

- **Active Listening:** Listen attentively to customer concerns, questions, and feedback to demonstrate empathy and understanding.

- **Clear Information:** Provide accurate and transparent information about products, services, pricing, and dealership policies.

- **Timely Responses:** Respond promptly to customer inquiries, whether in person, over the phone, or through digital channels.

Handling Customer Inquiries and Complaints

Efficiently addressing inquiries and complaints resolves issues and strengthens customer relationships:

- **Empowerment:** Empower frontline employees to resolve minor issues and escalate complex concerns as needed.
- **Problem-Solving Skills:** Equip employees with problem-solving skills to identify root causes and implement effective solutions.
- **Follow-Up:** Follow up with customers after issue resolution to ensure satisfaction and prevent recurrence.

Personalized Service Approaches

Personalization enhances the customer experience and builds loyalty:

- **Customer Profiling:** Use customer data and preferences to tailor recommendations, communications, and service offerings.
- **Relationship Building:** Establish personal connections with customers through personalized interactions and remembering their preferences.
- **Anticipate Needs:** Proactively anticipate customer needs based on past interactions and preferences.

Building Customer Loyalty

Loyalty programs and exceptional service foster long-term customer relationships:

- **Rewards and Incentives:** Offer loyalty rewards, discounts, and exclusive benefits for repeat customers.
- **Recognition:** Acknowledge loyal customers and express appreciation through personalized messages or special events.
- **Consistent Experience:** Ensure consistency in service quality across all customer touchpoints and interactions.

Leveraging Technology for Customer Service

Technology enhances efficiency and effectiveness in delivering customer service:

- **Customer Relationship Management (CRM) Systems:** Use CRM systems to track customer interactions, preferences, and purchase history.
- **Digital Communication:** Utilize email, SMS, and social media platforms for personalized communication and customer engagement.
- **Self-Service Options:** Offer online scheduling, service reminders, and FAQs to empower customers and streamline

processes.

Measuring Service Quality

Measuring service quality provides insights for improvement and performance evaluation:

- **Customer Feedback:** Solicit feedback through surveys, reviews, and customer satisfaction scores to assess service experiences.

- **Service Metrics:** Track metrics such as response times, resolution rates, and customer retention to monitor service effectiveness.

- **Benchmarking:** Compare service quality against industry standards and competitors to identify strengths and areas for improvement.

Employee Training and Development

Investing in employee training enhances skills and service delivery:

- **Product Knowledge:** Ensure employees have comprehensive knowledge of vehicles, features, and service offerings.

- **Customer Service Skills:** Provide training in active listening, empathy, conflict resolution, and effective communication.

- **Continuous Learning:** Offer ongoing training programs and development opportunities to keep employees updated on industry trends and best practices.

Continuous Improvement Strategies

Continuous improvement ensures ongoing excellence in customer service:

- **Root Cause Analysis:** Identify underlying causes of customer issues or complaints to implement preventive measures.
- **Quality Assurance:** Conduct regular audits and assessments to maintain service standards and compliance.
- **Innovation and Adaptation:** Stay agile and responsive to changing customer expectations, market trends, and technological advancements.

Conclusion

Delivering customer service excellence in automotive sales requires dedication, empathy, and a commitment to continuous improvement. By creating a customer-centric culture, fostering effective communication, handling inquiries and complaints with efficiency, personalizing service approaches, building customer loyalty, leveraging technology, measuring service quality, investing in employee training, and implementing strategies for continuous improvement, dealerships can differentiate themselves, enhance customer satisfaction, and drive business growth. Remember, every customer interaction is an opportunity to exceed expectations and build long-term relationships in the competitive automotive market.

Chapter 14: Digital Marketing Strategies for Automotive Sales

Digital marketing plays a crucial role in reaching and engaging automotive customers in today's competitive landscape. This chapter explores comprehensive strategies, techniques, and best practices to leverage digital marketing effectively for automotive sales.

Importance of Digital Marketing in Automotive Sales

Digital marketing enhances visibility, drives traffic, and generates leads for automotive dealerships:

- **Reach and Targeting:** Expand reach to a broader audience and target specific demographics, behaviors, and interests.

- **Engagement:** Foster engagement through interactive content, personalized experiences, and direct communication channels.
- **Measurable Results:** Track performance metrics and ROI to optimize campaigns and maximize marketing investments.

Website Optimization

Optimizing dealership websites enhances user experience and conversion rates:

- **User-Friendly Design:** Ensure intuitive navigation, fast loading times, and mobile responsiveness.
- **SEO Optimization:** Implement SEO best practices to improve search engine rankings and visibility.
- **Lead Capture Forms:** Use clear and compelling call-to-actions (CTAs) and lead capture forms to convert visitors into leads.

Search Engine Optimization (SEO)

SEO strategies improve organic search visibility and drive qualified traffic:

- **Keyword Research:** Identify relevant

keywords and phrases that potential customers use to search for automotive products and services.

- **On-Page Optimization:** Optimize meta tags, headings, content, and images with targeted keywords.

- **Link Building:** Build quality backlinks from reputable websites to improve domain authority and search rankings.

Paid Advertising (PPC)

PPC campaigns drive targeted traffic and maximize visibility in search engine results:

- **Google Ads:** Create targeted campaigns using keywords, demographics, and geographic targeting.

- **Display Ads:** Utilize visual ads on relevant websites and platforms to increase brand awareness and drive traffic.

- **Retargeting:** Retarget website visitors with personalized ads to encourage return visits and conversions.

Content Marketing

Content marketing establishes authority, educates customers, and nurtures leads:

- **Blog Posts:** Publish informative articles, how-to guides, and industry insights to attract and engage potential customers.
- **Video Marketing:** Create engaging video content showcasing vehicle features, customer testimonials, and dealership events.
- **Infographics:** Use visual content to convey complex information, statistics, and comparisons effectively.

Social Media Strategies

Social media platforms build brand presence, engage customers, and drive traffic:

- **Platform Selection:** Identify platforms where target audiences are active (e.g., Facebook, Instagram, LinkedIn) and tailor content accordingly.
- **Community Engagement:** Foster conversations, respond to comments and messages promptly, and encourage user-generated content.
- **Paid Social Ads:** Run targeted ad campaigns to reach specific demographics, promote offers, and drive conversions.

Email Marketing

Email marketing campaigns nurture leads, promote offers, and maintain customer relationships:

- **Segmentation:** Segment email lists based on demographics, behaviors, and purchase history for personalized messaging.
- **Automated Campaigns:** Set up automated workflows for welcome emails, follow-ups, and personalized recommendations.
- **Performance Tracking:** Monitor open rates, click-through rates (CTR), and conversions to optimize email content and campaigns.

Online Reputation Management

Managing online reviews and customer feedback enhances brand reputation and credibility:

- **Review Monitoring:** Monitor and respond to customer reviews on platforms like Google My Business, Yelp, and social media.
- **Customer Feedback:** Solicit feedback through surveys and use insights to improve customer service and dealership operations.
- **Positive Promotion:** Highlight positive reviews and testimonials on your website,

social media, and marketing materials.

Lead Generation Techniques

Effective lead generation strategies attract and convert potential customers into leads:

- **Incentives and Offers:** Offer incentives such as discounts, promotions, or free consultations to encourage lead generation.

- **Landing Pages:** Create dedicated landing pages with clear value propositions and compelling CTAs to capture leads.

- **Webinars and Events:** Host online webinars, virtual test drives, or live events to engage prospects and collect contact information.

Analytics and Metrics

Analyzing performance metrics provides insights for optimizing digital marketing strategies:

- **Google Analytics:** Track website traffic, user behavior, conversion rates, and ROI from different marketing channels.

- **Campaign Attribution:** Attribute conversions to specific marketing campaigns to determine effectiveness and allocate budgets.

- **A/B Testing:** Conduct experiments to test variations in ads, landing pages, and email campaigns to improve performance.

Integration with Traditional Marketing Efforts

Integrating digital marketing with traditional methods amplifies reach and enhances brand consistency:

- **Cross-Promotion:** Promote digital campaigns through traditional media channels such as print ads, radio, and direct mail.
- **Unified Brand Messaging:** Ensure consistent messaging, branding elements, and offers across all marketing channels.
- **Offline-to-Online Conversion:** Use QR codes, custom URLs, or promo codes in traditional ads to drive traffic to digital platforms.

Future Trends in Automotive Digital Marketing

Anticipated trends shaping the future of automotive digital marketing include:

- **AI and Machine Learning:** Use AI-driven insights to personalize customer experiences, predict buying behaviors, and optimize campaigns.

- **Voice Search Optimization:** Adapt SEO strategies for voice search queries and devices such as smart speakers and virtual assistants.

- **Augmented Reality (AR) and Virtual Reality (VR):** Implement AR/VR technologies for virtual vehicle tours, customization experiences, and interactive content.

Conclusion

Effective digital marketing strategies are essential for automotive dealerships to attract, engage, and convert customers in a competitive market. By optimizing websites, implementing SEO and PPC campaigns, leveraging content marketing and social media strategies, utilizing email marketing and online reputation management, employing effective lead generation techniques, analyzing metrics, integrating with traditional marketing efforts, and staying ahead of future trends, dealerships can enhance visibility, drive sales, and build lasting customer relationships. Remember, digital marketing provides powerful tools and opportunities to showcase dealership strengths, connect with customers, and achieve business growth in the dynamic automotive industry landscape.

Chapter 15: Finance and Insurance (F&I) Strategies in Automotive Sales

Finance and Insurance (F&I) departments play a crucial role in automotive sales by providing financing options, insurance products, and additional services to customers. This chapter explores comprehensive strategies, techniques, and best practices for optimizing F&I operations and enhancing customer satisfaction.

Importance of F&I in Automotive Sales

F&I departments contribute to dealership profitability and customer satisfaction through:

- **Revenue Generation:** Generating additional revenue through financing, insurance products, and aftermarket services.

- **Customer Convenience:** Offering one-stop shopping for vehicle purchase, financing, and protection plans.

- **Compliance:** Ensuring adherence to regulatory requirements and ethical practices in financial transactions.

Strategies for Maximizing Profitability

Effective strategies to maximize profitability in F&I departments include:

- **Product Portfolio:** Offer a diverse range of finance products, extended warranties, vehicle protection plans, and gap insurance to meet varying customer needs.

- **Upselling and Cross-Selling:** Identify opportunities to recommend additional products or services that enhance customer satisfaction and dealership revenue.

- **Profit Margin Management:** Optimize pricing strategies and profit margins while remaining competitive in the market.

Customer Education and Transparency

Educating customers about finance and insurance options builds trust and facilitates informed decision-making:

- **Clear Communication:** Explain finance terms, insurance coverage, and optional products in simple, understandable language.

- **Disclosure:** Provide transparent information about pricing, fees, interest rates, and terms to avoid misunderstandings or surprises.

- **Comparison Tools:** Offer tools or resources to help customers compare financing options, insurance coverage, and pricing.

Product Offerings and Customization

Tailoring finance and insurance offerings to customer preferences enhances satisfaction and loyalty:

- **Customization:** Customize financing terms, down payments, and insurance coverage options to align with customer budgets and preferences.
- **Bundle Packages:** Bundle multiple products (e.g., financing, extended warranty, maintenance plans) for added value and convenience.
- **Flexibility:** Offer flexible payment plans or refinancing options to accommodate changing customer needs.

Negotiation Tactics and Techniques

Negotiation skills are essential for achieving mutually beneficial agreements in F&I transactions:

- **Focus on Value:** Emphasize the value and benefits of finance products and insurance coverage to justify costs.

- **Alternative Solutions:** Present alternative financing options or insurance packages based on customer preferences and budget.
- **Objection Handling:** Address customer concerns or objections with clear explanations and options for resolution.

Compliance Considerations and Regulations

Adherence to legal and regulatory requirements is critical for F&I operations:

- **Regulatory Compliance:** Stay informed about federal, state, and local regulations governing finance, insurance, and consumer protection.
- **Ethical Practices:** Uphold ethical standards in advertising, pricing, disclosure, and customer interactions.
- **Training and Certification:** Ensure F&I managers and staff receive ongoing training and certification to maintain compliance and professionalism.

Evolving Role of F&I Managers

F&I managers play a multifaceted role in customer service, sales support, and compliance management:

- **Customer Advocacy:** Advocate for customer interests while achieving dealership objectives and revenue targets.

- **Technology Integration:** Utilize digital tools and platforms for streamlined paperwork, digital signatures, and remote transactions.

- **Data Analytics:** Analyze customer data, buying behaviors, and market trends to tailor F&I offerings and improve sales strategies.

Enhancing Customer Experience and Satisfaction

Delivering exceptional service and value fosters long-term customer relationships and satisfaction:

- **Post-Sale Support:** Provide ongoing support, assistance with claims, and follow-up on customer satisfaction with F&I products.

- **Feedback Loop:** Solicit feedback from customers to evaluate service quality, product effectiveness, and overall satisfaction.

- **Continuous Improvement:** Implement feedback and insights to refine F&I processes, product offerings, and customer interactions.

Emerging Trends in F&I

Future trends shaping the F&I landscape include:

- **Digital Transformation:** Embrace digital platforms for remote transactions, online financing applications, and virtual consultations.

- **Personalization:** Use data analytics and AI to personalize finance and insurance recommendations based on individual customer profiles.

- **Regulatory Changes:** Stay agile and adapt to evolving regulatory requirements impacting F&I practices and consumer protections.

Conclusion

Finance and Insurance strategies are integral to automotive sales success, profitability, and customer satisfaction. By implementing effective strategies for maximizing profitability, educating customers transparently, tailoring product offerings, mastering negotiation tactics, ensuring compliance with regulations, adapting to the evolving role of F&I managers, enhancing customer experience, and embracing emerging trends, dealerships can strengthen their F&I operations, build trust, and achieve sustainable growth in the competitive automotive market.

Remember, each F&I interaction is an opportunity to provide value, meet customer needs, and reinforce dealership reputation and integrity.

Chapter 16: Service Department Excellence in Automotive Sales

The service department is a critical component of automotive sales, providing maintenance, repairs, and customer support that contribute to customer satisfaction and dealership profitability. This chapter explores comprehensive strategies, techniques, and best practices for achieving excellence in service department operations.

Importance of Service Department Excellence

A well-managed service department enhances customer loyalty, generates revenue, and strengthens dealership reputation:

- **Customer Retention:** Maintain long-term relationships through reliable service and exceptional customer experiences.

- **Revenue Generation:** Generate revenue from service appointments, parts sales, and additional services.

- **Brand Reputation:** Uphold dealership reputation by delivering quality service and resolving customer issues effectively.

Service Department Operations

Efficient operations ensure timely service delivery and customer satisfaction:

- **Workflow Management:** Streamline service processes from appointment scheduling to vehicle delivery.

- **Resource Allocation:** Optimize technician schedules, equipment usage, and inventory management for maximum efficiency.

- **Workflow Integration:** Integrate service operations with other dealership departments for seamless customer experiences.

Customer Service Strategies

Customer-centric strategies enhance satisfaction and loyalty:

- **Appointment Convenience:** Offer flexible scheduling options, online booking, and express service lanes.

- **Communication Channels:** Provide clear communication through text updates, phone calls, or online portals.

- **Service Advisors:** Train service advisors to

provide personalized recommendations, address concerns, and ensure customer satisfaction.

Service Advisor Roles and Responsibilities

Service advisors play a pivotal role in customer interactions and service department efficiency:

- **Customer Engagement:** Build rapport, actively listen to customer concerns, and provide knowledgeable guidance.

- **Technical Knowledge:** Maintain up-to-date knowledge of vehicle systems, repairs, and maintenance schedules.

- **Conflict Resolution:** Resolve customer complaints or issues promptly and professionally.

Technician Training and Development

Continuous training enhances technician skills, efficiency, and service quality:

- **Technical Proficiency:** Provide ongoing training on new technologies, diagnostic tools, and repair techniques.

- **Certifications:** Support technicians in obtaining manufacturer certifications and specialized training.

- **Soft Skills:** Enhance communication skills, teamwork, and customer interaction capabilities.

Technology Integration in Service

Adopting technology improves service department efficiency and customer experiences:

- **Service Management Software:** Use integrated software for scheduling, work orders, parts inventory, and customer relationship management (CRM).
- **Diagnostic Tools:** Invest in advanced diagnostic equipment and software to expedite repairs and accuracy.
- **Digital Inspections:** Conduct digital vehicle inspections with photo and video documentation for transparency and customer education.

Service Marketing and Promotion

Effective marketing strategies drive service department visibility and customer engagement:

- **Promotional Campaigns:** Offer seasonal service specials, maintenance packages, and loyalty rewards programs.
- **Customer Education:** Provide informative content on vehicle maintenance tips,

service benefits, and common repair issues.

- **Referral Programs:** Incentivize customer referrals with discounts or rewards for new service appointments.

Quality Assurance and Performance Metrics

Monitoring service quality ensures consistency and customer satisfaction:

- **Service Quality Standards:** Establish benchmarks for service excellence and adherence to manufacturer guidelines.
- **Customer Feedback:** Gather feedback through surveys, reviews, and service satisfaction scores to identify areas for improvement.
- **Performance Metrics:** Track key metrics such as service turnaround time, first-time fix rate, and customer retention rates.

Managing Customer Expectations

Setting realistic expectations fosters trust and satisfaction:

- **Clear Communication:** Communicate service timelines, costs, and expectations upfront to manage customer expectations.
- **Transparency:** Provide updates on service

progress, additional repairs, and costs before proceeding with work.

- **Resolution of Issues:** Address any delays or complications promptly and offer solutions to mitigate customer inconvenience.

Upselling Opportunities

Identifying upselling opportunities enhances revenue without compromising customer trust:

- **Maintenance Reminders:** Recommend preventative maintenance services based on vehicle age, mileage, and service history.

- **Additional Services:** Offer optional services such as detailing, tire rotations, or windshield treatments during service visits.

- **Educational Approach:** Educate customers on the benefits of recommended services for vehicle performance, safety, and longevity.

Handling Complaints and Resolving Issues

Effective complaint resolution preserves customer relationships and dealership reputation:

- **Empowerment:** Equip service advisors with authority to resolve issues and satisfy customer concerns.

- **Follow-Up:** Follow up with customers post-service to ensure satisfaction and address any lingering concerns.
- **Continuous Improvement:** Use feedback from complaints to implement process improvements and prevent future issues.

Fostering a Culture of Continuous Improvement

Encouraging innovation and learning enhances service department effectiveness:

- **Feedback Mechanisms:** Encourage staff and customer feedback to identify opportunities for improvement.
- **Training and Development:** Invest in ongoing training programs, certifications, and skills development for service personnel.
- **Benchmarking and Best Practices:** Benchmark against industry standards and adopt best practices to optimize service operations.

Conclusion

Achieving service department excellence requires meticulous planning, effective management, and a commitment to customer satisfaction. By optimizing service department operations, implementing customer service strategies, empowering service advisors, investing in technician training, integrating technology, marketing services effectively, ensuring quality assurance, managing customer expectations, seizing upselling opportunities, handling complaints professionally, and fostering a culture of continuous improvement, dealerships can differentiate themselves, build loyalty, and drive long-term success in the competitive automotive market. Remember, exceptional service experiences not only retain customers but also attract new business through positive word-of-mouth and reputation enhancement.

Conclusion

In the dynamic world of automobile sales, excellence isn't just a goal; it's the cornerstone of success. Throughout this book, we've explored every facet of the automotive sales process, from mastering the art of customer interaction to leveraging digital strategies, from navigating finance and insurance intricacies to optimizing service department operations. Each chapter has been a journey into the heart of what it takes to thrive in this competitive industry.

Customer-Centric Approach: At the heart of every successful automotive sale is a deep understanding of customer needs, preferences, and aspirations. By adopting a customer-centric approach, dealerships can build trust, foster long-term relationships, and create memorable experiences that extend beyond the showroom.

Digital Innovation: The digital landscape has revolutionized how we connect with customers and market vehicles. Embracing digital marketing, social media strategies, and advanced analytics not only expands reach but also personalizes interactions, driving engagement and conversion in an increasingly digital world.

Finance and Insurance Expertise: The finance and insurance (F&I) department is pivotal in closing deals and enhancing profitability. By offering transparent options, educating customers, and adhering to regulatory standards, F&I professionals not only secure transactions but also build confidence and loyalty.

Service Excellence: The service department is the backbone of customer satisfaction and retention. From efficient operations to personalized service, ongoing training, and technological integration, service excellence ensures that every customer interaction reinforces dealership reputation and trust.

Continuous Improvement: In a constantly evolving industry, the commitment to continuous improvement sets apart successful dealerships. By listening to feedback, embracing innovation, and adapting to market trends, dealerships can stay ahead, deliver exceptional experiences, and drive sustainable growth.

As we conclude this journey through automotive sales training, remember that success lies not just in the transactions made, but in the relationships built and the trust earned. By embodying the principles of excellence, integrity, and innovation, dealerships can navigate challenges, seize opportunities, and thrive in the ever-changing automotive landscape.

Here's to a future where every dealership excels, every customer delights, and the spirit of innovation continues to drive the automotive sales industry forward.

www.ingramcontent.com/pod-product-compliance
Lightning Source LLC
Chambersburg PA
CBHW060856170526
45158CB00001B/377